THE HERB MAGIC SPELL BOOK

A BEGINNER'S GUIDE FOR SPELLS FOR LOVE,
HEALTH, WEALTH, AND MORE

BRIDGET BISHOP

HENTOPAN
PUBLISHING

HENTOPAN
PUBLISHING

CONTENTS

Get this additional book free just for joining the Hentopan Launch Squad.

If you want insider access, plus this free book, all you have to do is scan the code below with your phone!

INTRODUCTION

I was introduced to herb magic by a witch friend, and it took me a long time to learn how to use each herb correctly and how different herbs can work together. I wrote this book to make it easier for beginners to get started. As I learned what worked, I added to my Book of Shadows, from which the spells in this book are drawn. I now have an extensive collection of herbs in my pantry that I have grown or collected myself. I love spending time in my magic garden and walking in the woods to gather herbs. The walks and the garden make me feel much more connected to the world around me. This book will show you how to use herbs that you may already have in your kitchens for personal care, healing, rituals, spiritual practices, and spells. You will learn spells, notes of caution, recipes, their magical correspondences, and lore for each herb. Also, you will learn how to combine herbs with crystals, candles, colors, elemental energies, and more, for powerful magical workings. From arrowroot to turmeric and elixirs to incense, this valuable guide to herbal magic is designed to help you broaden your magic and spellcraft for a more magical and natural life.

The history of herbs, plants, and herbal magic is discussed to provide an interpretation guide for herbal magic. Various herbal spells, rituals, and methodologies are outlined, so you can incorporate them into your daily life and create a mystical herbal environment where your spells can be manifested. Each spell provides instruction on how to communicate your intentions within and throughout your use of herbs and using your intuition to interpret findings to discover the beautiful relationships we have with worlds beyond our own. Natural elements coupled with herbs are a considerable component of practicing witchcraft. Practitioners of herbal magic have been doing research and practicing the craft since the beginning of humankind. I am sure the plants and the elements were communicating with each other long before that.

A potion, ritual, charm, or spell is only as good as its ingredients. Many people have come to use herbal remedies, essential oils, and crystals for unblocking and balancing the chakras, raising spiritual vibrations, astral projection, and providing offerings to deities, along with the various intentions for each spell. Herbs and their oils are used to gain information from our subconscious mind and the spiritual realms. By using essential herbs in your spells, you can direct very specific energies towards your intentions for healing, love, prosperity, personal growth, luck, happiness, travel, retirement, and other rituals and magical traditions, of which there are too many to name.

Considering this is a book of spells, it's evident that many items, materials, and ingredients go into the art of magic. Rosemary, ginger, lemon balm, cayenne, sage, salt, garlic, and basil are just a few of the common herbal ingredients explained in detail for your information gathering. Essential herbs are used to amplify and enhance the magic of these spells. Herbs can be used in rituals, as talismans, incorporated into amulets and sachets, and even to anoint our physical bodies. In addition, they are also used to create powerful witchcraft goods. Our ancestors documented during medieval times that prayers were uttered for summoning guardian angels, and incantations were cast to ward off illnesses. Herbs such as rosemary have a long, rich history of being used to remember the dead and to enhance clarity and memory. So you will see many valuable rosemary tips as you read on. In fact, Shakespeare wrote of the memory-enhancing powers of rosemary in his plays *Romeo and Juliet* and *Hamlet*. Combining specific phrases, specialized rhymes, symbolic items, and herbs is far from unique to the Anglo-Saxon world. I consider my incantations the interlocutor of herbs acting together in a desired way to bring me my desired effects. To use the magic of herbs you need a knowledge of their properties, what they do, and how to use them properly. I wrote this book on herbal magic as a guide to connect you with the traditions, correspondences, and healing magic of various herbs and how they can bring better health and wellness, light, happiness, and love into your life. Please enjoy!

PART 1:

UNDERSTANDING HERB MAGIC

It is easy to underestimate the power of herbs in healing magic. People tend to go directly to over-the-counter manufactured medicines to treat inflammation, headaches, and indigestion because we have been conditioned all of our lives to depend on prescription or commercial drugs. The beautiful thing about herbs is that they are not formulated. They are provided by Mother Earth and nurtured by water, sun, and all that is natural in this world. You can choose an herb here and choose an herb there and have healing powers in the truest sense of the phrase. Each part of a plant has special and significant properties, so my primary objective in Part 1 is to teach you about them. Magic Herbs come from the leaves, roots, petals, and stems of special plants that can be used for healing magic, charging, and cleansing objects, or you can simply consume their magical properties. This half of the book is meant to explain how herb magic works, which is useful before jumping right into the spell work in Part 2.

THE MAGIC OF HERBS

Originally, there was no difference between "magic" and medicine. Now we recognize that medicine works on the physical, and magic works on the spiritual level. Without the lore of European magic, medicine and science could never have developed successfully. The evidence of the critical role magic has played in the origins of modern medicine is overwhelming. In order to understand the role magic has played in medicine, we have to be aware of the differences between the magic of a thousand years ago and what it has evolved into today. The magic at the beginning of the 20th century, referred to as natural magic, was predominately based on the belief that God created this world and that every individual component was not only connected but that correspondences between creatures in one part of the continuous chain corresponded to elements or creatures in another part of this unbroken chain in God's creation, with the purpose being the underlying belief.

Nothing was done in vain by Nature or God. Therefore, there is a purpose for everything. The belief was that God left clues as to those correspondences, such as the human brain and the flesh of a walnut in its shell. It was assumed that occult powers were part of these correspondences, and that was the reason they could affect each other. The magician's role was to identify the correspondences and their precise magical effect, so they could then be put to use.

Just as magic has been a part of scientific history, healing with herbs is as old as humankind itself. The relationship between humanity and our quest for medicine in nature dates back thousands of years. It is evidenced by historical documents, original herbal medicines, and preserved monuments (plants in their own right have become supreme documents that have to be preserved). Awareness of the use of herbs in medicine comes from years and years of fighting against illness and disease, which led man to pursue drugs in leaves, bark, seeds, fruit, and other plant parts. Present-day pharmacotherapy has accepted the active ingredients in herbs and has included many in modern medicine, including a broad range of medications of plant origin; information that was known to ancient peoples and used throughout millennia.

Herbal Magic on a Global Perspective

Herbal magic is an ancestral and traditional practice, especially for healing, and has many global origins. Witches and plants have converged naturally with provincial cultural beliefs and norms, seasonal patterns, health concerns, and community needs, gathering together to learn, discuss, and provide feedback to others about their magical experiences with herbs. Many people who live in plant-based cultures are natives. Also, in many developing countries, traditional herbal medicine is still the main source of healthcare, according to the World Health Organization (WHO).[1]

The use of herbs in healing cross-culturally has grown significantly in the past fifty years. It is now a very popular alternative medicine method and a profitable market for the health and wellness industry. Many people use healing herbs in their daily healthcare regimens through potions, elixirs, teas, culinary preparations, supplements, and tinctures. In addition, many mainstream medical practitioners add herbal medicines to their conventional protocols as a form of preventative medicine and treatment for chronic conditions. This magical renaissance has given way to an unprecedented relationship of herbalism as extensive historical lore, the world of healing magic, and a scientifically proven form of treatment in modern-day global capitalism.

Herbs and the Elements

Water, Air, Fire, and Earth are the four elements that make up the basic components of the Universe. All that is between the Earth and the spiritual realms is composed of one or a combination of these four elements. Many magical practitioners consider Spirit to be a fifth element that exists within the four elements. When it comes to incense burning in the Air or anointing with an herb, we draw directly upon the energies of the Elements to achieve our goal. To achieve the highest potency, get to know your element before working with something from its realm. The most basic manifestations of the elements come from nature. Earth can be a handful of soil, a leaf blowing in the wind for Air, a river flowing for Water, and an ember for Fire.

Many herbs correspond with the elements, and each element corresponds to a specific magical outcome:

EARTH promotes grounding, peace, business, stability, green growth, fertility, and employment. Herbs corresponding with Earth include:

Bisort	Honeysuckle	Fern	Mugwort
Oakmoss	Primrose	Rhubarb	Magnolia
Horehound	Patchouly	Vetivert	Vervain

AIR promotes freedom, divination, eloquence, intuition, travel, wisdom, intellect, and communication. Herbs corresponding with Air include:

Almond	Peppermint	Sage	Lemongrass
Lavender	Benzoin	Lemon Verbena	Mace
Marjoram	Star Anise	Marjoram	Acacia

WATER promotes peace, relaxation, psychism, healing, compassion, dreams, friendship, and reconciliation. The herbs corresponding with Water include:

Apple Blossom	Cherry	Lemon	Iris
Liquorice	Sweet Pea	Eucalyptus	Comfrey
Vanilla	Peach	Orchid	Sandalwood
Lilly	Elder	Tansy	Ylang-Ylang
Thyme	Coconut	Catnip	Lemon Balm
Camphor	Orris	Jasmine	Stephanotis
Spearmint	Plumeria	Violet	Hyacinth

FIRE promotes courage, passion, purification, magical power, defensive magic, and physical strength. Herbs corresponding with Fire include:

Basil	Dill	Nutmeg	Rose Geranium
Juniper	Lime	Marigold	Grains of Paradise
Sassafras	Peppermint	Fennel	Frankincense
Orange	Cinnamon	Carnation	Dragon's Blood
Garlic	Woodruff	Galangal	Angelica
Heliotrope	Coriander	Rosemary	Deer's Tongue

Why Herbs are a Great Place to Start with Magic

I am doing my happy dance when I blend spices and herbs and add a bit of magic! To start your own collection, all you need to do is gather some seeds, leaves, berries, bark, and a few bottles to concoct powerful ingredients to add to your spellwork. As a real-life practitioner of herbal magic, I am happy to provide you with great recipes, great spells, and overall great magic as you continue your journey through this book. Here are some steps for you to start on your path toward herbal magic:

TOUCH, SMELL, TASTE:

Crush your herbs and then rub them together and smell. Practice naming herbs and spices without looking at labels, or blindfold yourself and get together with family and friends and take turns guessing what the herb is using only smell and touch. Envelop yourself in the experience of the aroma. Create a collection of sacred tins and jars. Put your magic into selecting the container for each herb. Cleanse with sage (of course, you want to cleanse with an herb). Design and creatively enhance your labels, making some for whole herbs and some for your magical blends.

TWO HERBAL MAGIC RULES:

1. The oils in spices and herbs dissipate or can go bad after a while, so it is best to start with whole spices and grind them yourself as needed. You can buy the following pre-ground: garlic, cinnamon, turmeric, and

sumac. Throw away any old spices you have that were pre-ground.

2. When starting out, use tried and true recipes and experiment with your own later, after learning how to combine your herbs and in what ratios. After making some blends from expertly written recipes, start using your own creativity, and herbal blending will soon become second nature.

PRACTICE:

The classic method for grinding herbs and making your own spices is by using a mortar and pestle. However, you can use an electric spice grinder for wizardry results. Here are some excellent methods for you to play with:

- Toast your spices before grinding.
- Smell after you grind your herbs.
- Add a little salt to your blend (great for popcorn).
- Don't rush. Enjoy the process; make sure you have allotted extra time for concocting.
- Keep your ground herbs and spice blends where you can see them so you remember to use them.
- Use them up within a couple of months.

2

HERB MAGIC BASICS

When we talk about herb magic, we may be referring to herbs, flowers, or even roots. All witches honor wild things and use ingredients given to us by the Earth. It is believed that herbs are probably the oldest known instruments of magic. Before the separation of medicine and magic, most healing practices were accomplished with herbal concoctions, prayer, and rituals. In modern times, a steaming cup of tea concocted with herbs can have emotional, spiritual, and nutritional benefits. Herbs are symbolic of the magical powers of the Elements. They begin as seeds of the Earth, where they are provided with nourishing minerals, and then interact with Fire (sunlight). From this phase, carbon dioxide is converted to oxygen by consorting with Air. Air in the form of breezes and wind scatters the seeds and continues the circle of life. All of these phases cannot take place without Water. Plants are critical to the Earth's water cycle as they purify and help the movement of the soil into the atmosphere.

Here lies the great illustration of how the Elements correspond with herbs. Plants are living beings and communicate with their plant neighbors through their roots, pollen, exchanging minerals, vibrations, and in other mystical ways. Plant intelligence is the subject of many research projects these days. Growing your own herbs, berries, flowers, and plants will help you commune with the Elements and the insect and animal world. Herbs are versatile and very useful in the practice of magic. Keep them in sachets, spell jars, as talismans, and other charms used for your magical workings. Spellwork transfers the energy of the herbs into a form we can use to bring our intentions into the world!

Doctrine of Signature

We can learn a great deal just by looking closely at plants. Learning about the climate, local habitats, hydrology, soils, and wildlife will enrich your magic in many wonderful ways. For instance, rich dark leaves indicate that a plant may do well in soil that is sandy or may be able to endure periods of drought. Plants that are picky about access to their berries grow thorns. And flowers that smell badly rely on insects that feed on carrion to spread their seeds. For millennia, people have used the appearance of plants to divine their magical properties. The "Doctrine of Signatures" is a broad concept depicting the plant's features resembling a body part or condition that the herb can treat. Hence, scarlet roots can heal problems of the heart or blood. Ginseng root is used to aid male sexual vitality because it resembles male genitalia. The spotted leaves of lungwort are thought to resemble a diseased lung; these are all examples of the Doctrine of Signature. The herbs' common names are often associated with their signature. In medieval times, magicians believed that God created signatures when creating plants to communicate to people how to use them.

Creating Your Altar

You don't have to be at an altar to cast a spell, but creating sacred space with your altar is a great place to focus your intentions, energy and practice your craft. You can set your altar up anywhere your intuition tells you. I was drawn to a window in my bedroom, facing the west, where the sun sets. I also have one in my office next to my desk. Having an altar somewhere it cannot be disturbed is important because spells work for as long as you have corresponding items in a sacred space. Every witch has their own unique journey, so be sure you feel connected spiritually to your altar and anything that comes into contact with it. Cloths are placed on an altar (usually) to keep them clean. Choosing an altar cloth is also part of your craft. It is a magical procedure, and you can use anything to which you feel drawn. I believe in using natural items, such as silk or bamboo. Here are some ideas for the color you may want to choose for your cloth:

- Red corresponds with Fire, and its magical properties include passion, courage, willpower, love, and desire.

- Green corresponds with Earth, and its magical properties include money, health, fertility, luck, abundance, and nature.
- Yellow corresponds with Air, and its magical properties include happiness, intelligence, clarity, and memory.
- Blue corresponds with Water, and its magical properties include spirituality, wisdom, calmness, and relaxation.
- Pink corresponds with Fire, and its magical properties include nurturing, romance, friendship, and healing.
- Orange corresponds with Fire, and its magical properties include justice, sexuality, buying property, emotions, and intellect.
- Brown corresponds with Earth, and its magical properties include cooking, animals, grounding, gardening, and nature.
- Purple corresponds with Spirit, and its magical properties include sexuality, balance, love, and acceptance.
- White corresponds with Air, and its magical properties include clarity, light, peace, cleansing, and inspiration.
- Gold corresponds with Fire, and its magical properties include wealth, enlightenment, fame, and fortune.
- Silver corresponds with Water, and its magical properties include dreams, intuition, telepathy, and astral projection.

Include items or symbols attributed to what you are honoring. I have five candles, one for each of the four directions and one in the middle. They can also be representing the Elements. I fill a clear crystal bowl with blessed water. When I first started, I had a glass bowl with spring water, and it was fantastic magic. As time went on, my interests and intentions grew. Here are some suggestions as to how you can honor the Elements on your altar:

- Air - East: Windchimes, feathers, incense, magnifying glass, knife
- Water - West: Rocks, crystal ball, water bowl, driftwood, seaweed, salt
- Earth - North: Herbs, seeds, bones, soil, bonsai
- Fire - South: Candles, orange, yellow, red crystals and flowers, lava stones, cactus, spicy foods, lighter or matches

When getting ready to start working magic in your kitchen, an altar is the best place to begin. While the kitchen itself is a sacred space, having an altar for spellwork can be useful. It is totally up to you how far you want to go with your kitchen altar, and it depends on the amount of space you have and how extensive your magic methods are. Some practitioners have a special place on their countertop, which is helpful unless you have limited counter space. You can make hanging altars, place crystals and tea candles on the back of your stove, or hang wall decorations with small shelves. Wall shelves come in handy in small kitchens. Once you get into it, you will find your whole kitchen is somewhat of a functioning altar, with magical tools, a blessed stovetop, and magical herbs lighting up your life.

Creating a Workspace in Your Kitchen for Herbs

Whether you grew up in a small family or a large family, the kitchen is usually the heart of the home. In my family, people seem to gravitate towards the kitchen. It seems to be where people bond and socialize while smelling the aromas of what is about to bring them together. This sense of togetherness is part of the magic that happens in the kitchen. It can take on a life of its own and lead to traditions and rituals that spring from daily living. These traditions and rituals often form the foundation of a witch's energy when it comes to herbal magic. Some people scoff at traditional domestic folk magic in a kitchen setting, but this type of magic has deep power woven into the fabric of our lives. After all, what could be more important than family, community, food, and a sacred place that provides all three?

Since we use herbs in almost every dish we make, it is important to realize how their potent energies match their potent flavors. Adding a few herbs to anything takes it up a notch in beautiful ways while at the same time intermingling your magical intent into your dish. As previously discussed, start by adding basic herbs, then as you learn more, start pairing energies and flavors together. Look to the corresponding colors and elements list provided and match them to your intentions and your herbs or blends. The spices and herbs work differently for different people because everyone has their own unique vibrations. Some herbs work better for me than others. For instance, I always have great luck with basil, while sometimes my spells fall flat with rosemary. Needless to say, I use a lot of basil. Figuring out which herbs work best for you can greatly improve your spellwork. While it isn't mandatory, growing your own herbs, knowing the seasons that are best for growing each particular herb where you live, and learning how to work conjointly with your kitchen's spirits, as well as the spirits in your hometown, can add a great depth to your herbal magic. Spellwork transfers the energy of the herbs into a form we can use to bring our intentions into the world.

How to Grow Your Own Herbs

Step 1: Choose your containers. Choose pots or containers that you can move from your kitchen to your porch or outside and back to your kitchen and altar. Clay, metal, resin, or wood; it is up to your intuition. Just make sure there is an escape route for water drainage. Also, size matters! Pick a pot that matches the size of the herb's growth you want to achieve. If the plant is in too big of a container, it will spend too much energy growing its roots. If a plant is cramped in a planter, it can become stressed out and die.

Step 2: Picking your herbs. If you are new to growing herbs, start simple. Basil, parsley, and mint are perfect for the new herbal magician. They lend themselves perfectly to frequent harvesting. Here are some other examples of herb choices and their properties:

- Mint: Grows aggressively, so it should be in an above-ground pot and does well with direct sunlight, but can do okay with some shade.
- Basil: Grows easily and needs to be well-watered. Use rich soil and provide direct sunlight.
- Parsley: Can grow with partial shade and does best in soil that is moist but well-drained.
- Oregano: Needs good drainage and full sunshine but does not do well in cold temperatures.
- Thyme: Needs less water, just moistened soil, and direct sunlight.
- Rosemary: Moisten the soil for the highly aromatic leaves of your rosemary plant. Do not leave it outdoors during winter months.
- Sage: Avoid planting it near cucumber (it affects the taste), but you can plant it near rosemary and cabbage. It needs well-drained soil and full direct sunlight.

Step 3: Start your herbal garden with starter plants. It will save you weeks of growing time and gives you a better chance of having a successful harvest.

Step 4: Choose the right soil, such as potting soil. Potting soil makes for better drainage than garden soil. Potting soil is porous and lighter, and gardening soil traps in moisture and is dense.

Step 5: Harvesting and caring for your herbs means watering them regularly. Harvest them sooner rather than later, as it will prime them for new growth.

Tools You'll Need for Your Herb Garden

1. Planters
2. Watering can
3. Fertilizer
4. Transplanter
5. Pruner
6. Labels
7. Grow light
8. Starter plants
9. Potting soil
10. Trowel

Enchanting Your Herbal Garden Tools

Enchanting or consecrating your herbal garden tools is the same as blessing your altar, crystals, candles, water, etc. Don't stop with just your garden tools. Enchant your cast iron skillet too. Just make sure to include your intent in all of your enchanting spells. Here are a few suggestions about how to make your garden tools magical:

- Get yourself a wood burner for a variety of magical needs. Burn symbols, sigils, words, and names into your spoons or potters.

- Draw a corresponding sigil with white chalk on the bottom of your cauldron or cast-iron prior to seasoning them.
- Burn your herbs like incense to enchant the whole kitchen and all of the utensils.
- Enchant your knives with protection spells and for sharpness.
- Keep clear quartz crystals near your herbs for overall powerful magic.

3

THE WHEEL OF THE YEAR

The Wheel of the Year represents the eight Wiccan and Neo-Paganism religious celebrations. It includes a celebration for the four solar festivals and the changing seasons: Fall equinox, summer solstice, spring equinox, and the winter solstice. The ancient Celts considered time cyclical. People are born and die, seasons change. However, everything comes again in some form or another, and naturally, the cycle repeats. In modern times, the Wheel of the Year helps pagans and witches keep balanced in an uncertain world. A scholarly mythologist named Jacob Grimm (1835) coined the term, and the Wiccan movement fixed the term in the 1950s. A core value of all pagan religions is to become aligned with nature. Celebrating the dates in the Wheel of the Year is meant to encourage a harmonious lifestyle with nature, not against it. In order to not depend on a predetermined beginning and end, the Wheel of the Year is a nonlinear arrangement of time. It's important to be in tune with what grows when in your local area and how that connects you to the earth and grounds you. Herbs and their folklore are an essential part of almost every pagan religion. Specifically, many of the Sabbats correspond with the magical properties of different herbs. The Wheel of the Year holy days include:

SAMHAIN

Samhain is a pagan religious festival to welcome the dark half of the year and hail the harvest's coming. Samhain celebrates the breaking down of the barriers between the physical world and the spirit world, bringing forth better interactions between humans and residents of the Otherworld.

Holiday: Halloween

Herbs:

Rosemary: Rosemary is a fantastic smudge for clearing and protection of all things sacred. Burn it for good health and vitality in the new year. Create a rosemary charm sachet to bring good people to you, and then blend it with thyme for the power to see them. It is also traditionally used at funerals to honor death as the great renewal of life. It has been said that rosemary is associated with women's culture and that it grows by houses where women are in charge. So, it should be no surprise that I have rosemary growing in front of my home! A ritual rosemary bath is a great way to prepare for Samhain.

Mugwort: Mugwort provokes visionary states by trance or dream. Use in teas and sachet charms for a ritual for the rites of

Artemis. This charm will bring justice to wrongdoers and healing to those who have been harmed. I use it infused in water with wormwood to wash my crystal balls and scrying mirrors for blessings. Put a bit in your shoes to protect you from weariness.

Sage: Sage protects during Samhain and works to enhance wisdom for the new year and bring prosperity. Its magical properties also include longevity, fertility, and protection for pregnancy.

St. John's Wort: Removes negativity, protection, alleviates anxiety and depression. Worn to protect against mental illness and dried over fire and placed in windows to ward off necromancers, ghosts and to protect the family from lightning, fire, and misfortune. Drives away all that is evil in preparation for Samhain.

Chamomile: Used in teas to promote sleep and reduce anxiety. Drink before a spell casting or ritual to break curses and bring prosperity. Chamomile will entice a lover, promote well-being and happiness, bring sweet dreams, and regenerate spirituality.

Crystals: Bloodstone, Black Obsidian, Carnelian, Jet, Crystal Quartz, Onyx, and Jet.

Earth Event: Scorpio

Date: October 31

Occasion: Celebration of the dead; cleaning and releasing

YULE

The rebirth of the sun follows the longest night of the year. Yule symbolizes the newly-born solstice sun or the "Great God." What could represent Yule better than hauling an evergreen in from the woods and adorning it with ornaments and lights? Fir, cedar, juniper, and pine trees offer protection, prosperity, the life cycle, and rebirth as magical properties. Maybe you have noticed, when all of the trees lay down for the winter, the evergreen remains green. What better portrayal for the continuation of life?

Holiday: Christmas

Herbs:

Cinnamon: During ancient times, cinnamon was used as a preservative and an expensive flavoring agent in meats. During the 1st century A.D., it was worth ten times the equivalent weight of silver. Cinnamon sticks are made from evergreen bark. Very often, what you are buying in the store is not "true" cinnamon, but cassia. They are both from the same species. Use it in incense, teas, and potions for increased clarity and magical powers. Cinnamon correspondence with Yule is evident by its warmth. Use it to anoint your broom and use it for cleansing as it has antimicrobial actions.

Ginger: Ginger is my favorite! Nothing speaks Yule like gingerbread. It makes a wonderfully magical tea, too! Basically, this particular plant has one thing directly in common with Yuletide. It was not a Christmas herb until the 1700s. Ginger corresponds with the sun and Mars, and its magical properties include love, health, money, grounding, and creativity. It also is great for digestion. Ginger symbolizes the promise of beginnings; the new year. Make some gingerbread cookies, and the whole world smiles.

Peppermint: Peppermint is a hybrid of spearmint and watermint that occurred naturally in the mid-1600s. Obviously, the world is familiar with the correspondence between Yule and peppermint as it is symbolized around the world in the form of candy canes. Originally, they were given to children in the 1800s to keep them quiet during Christmas church services.

Nutmeg: Nutmeg comes from the evergreen tree, which also produces mace. Until recent times, both were very expensive. Back in the 1300s, one pound of nutmeg had the same value as one cow. It was only available from one South Pacific island until the British began growing it in other regions. Believe it or not, nutmeg, along with cinnamon and clove, was the source of wars being fought, as it was used in mincemeat preparations during the 12 days of Christmas. It corresponds with the element Fire, and its magical properties include fidelity, luck, money, and good health. Consider using nutmeg for your oaths rituals. ***WARNING: Nutmeg can be toxic in very large quantities, so season with good sense.

Crystals: Blue Calcite, Garnet, Fuchsite, Moss Agate, and Clear Quartz

Earth Event: Winter solstice: Capricorn

Date: December 20-25

Occasion: Fellowship, song, candlelight, and lighting the sacred fire

IMBOLC (BRIGID'S DAY)

Imbolc symbolizes pregnancy, the start of the lambing season, and the beginning of spring. It is associated with the earth awakening, hidden potential, the stirring of life, and the promise of renewal. It is a time to look forward and let go of the past. Spring cleaning is in the air, making room for new beginnings. This can be manifested by clearing your heart and mind, making wishes and making commitments, as well as cleaning your home. Brigid was the Celtic Goddess of poetry, smithcraft, and healing, and was such a part of the Christian faith, she was entitled St. Brigid. As the Fire Goddess of the Sun, she offers fertility to the people and the land. She is deeply connected to newborns and midwives. In the Wiccan religion, she is the Triple Goddess, but in her Maiden aspect at Imbolc.

Holiday: Candlemas

Herbs:

Angelica: Angelica is associated with the angels Gabriel and Michael. It corresponds with the sun and the element Fire.

Magically it is used for protection against evil and for breaking hexes. It also has blessing properties, and you can grow it yourself to protect your garden and home. Added to a sachet or amulet, it will ward off evil spirits and illness, thereby increasing longevity. Take it with you as a talisman if you want to gamble. Added to a ritual bath, it is a great spell breaker. If your home needs to be exorcised, Angelica is the herb for the job. Burning the leaves is known to stimulate visions and enhance clairvoyance.

Heather: Heather provides us with the ability to see reality for what it is and to do so objectively. Bees love heather, symbolizing positive community living. Bees have long been associated with social order and communal living, with each bee having a clearly defined role, but the hive is viewed as a single organism rather than as thousands of individual bees. It symbolizes sacrifice and self-control. Heather's magical properties include enthusiasm, conjuring ghosts, making rain, sensuality, self-expression, and the possible consequences of unbridled passion. Heather's association with Imbolc helps us to understand the magic behind the holiday. Wear it for good luck. If you want to be visited by a loved one who has passed, at midnight, pick a sprig of heather and place it in some blessed water, and put it in the darkest corner of your home. Meditate on your lost loved one, and it is said their shadow will appear.

Celandine: Celandine represents a time for planting the first seeds, a time of hope for warmer days to come. Sheep, while impregnated, began to produce milk, which was a sign of spring approaching. Celandine aids in getting you out of a bind and in escaping any type of unwarranted imprisonment or entrapment. Every three days, place a new piece next to your skin, and any depression will be lifted. It is also a court-spell herb, in case you need to win the favor of a jury or judge. Celandine's power frees the mind of depression and will detoxify the liver and blood. It is also suggested to those suffering from cataracts.

Blackberry: The berries and the leaves of the blackberry bush are sacred to Imbolc and are used for healing and prosperity. One method for enhancing your spellwork is to sprinkle blackberry into a candle flame during your ritual. This adds more power to your spells. Use the leaves in your rituals for prosperity or add to an elixir for protection. I carry it in a charm pouch for its healing properties, and I love adding blackberry to my bathwater.

Crystals: Amethyst, Peridot, Moss Agate, Onyx, Selenite, Moonstone, and Sunstone

Earth Event: Midway between the winter solstice and the spring equinox: Aquarius

Date: February 1

Occasion: Celebration for the Earth Goddess's recovery postpartum, Lunar Fire Festivals Day of Feast, Earth Goddess gives birth

OSTRA (LADY DAY; BACCHANALIA)

The Wheel of the Year's second spring festival (in between Imbolc and Beltane) is a celebration of the equilibrium between extremes that happen during the seasons. It is the official start of spring and the exact moment of balance between the dark and the light. The days growing longer is symbolic of the transition of God from infancy into maturity. As the temperature warms upon the Earth, it becomes more fertile, and with that, greener, and buds start to blossom. Just writing about the buds starting to blossom gives me goosebumps. The bees start to pollinate as winter is past and being outside is enjoyable again. The heat of summer is yet to come, so this is the time for enjoying the equinox and its balanced energies.

Holiday: Easter

Herbs:

Lemongrass: For centuries, this herb has been used for healing. Lemongrass has been used historically for its oils. In the 1600s, it was shipped as a perfume around the world. People of great wealth anointed themselves with the precious oil to cover their own bodily smells. Medicinally, it helps relieve digestive issues, lower fevers, and provides antimicrobial and antibacterial properties. Magically, it aids in openness and communication, protection, love, and luck.

Spearmint: This is used for healing, love, and protection while sleeping. Burning spearmint works magically for healing respiratory illness. Carry it in a sachet for overall health and wellness, or use it in a ritual bath while enjoying its aromatic qualities. For wishing spells, write your intention on a piece of paper and wrap it in spearmint leaves. Wrap in a piece of red material, sew it closed with red thread, and keep it in a sacred place. Your wish will be granted by the time its smell has dissipated. Its magical properties affect dreams, relaxation, transformation, exorcism, animals, spirit offering, and protection against intruders and dangers. Spearmint is also advantageous to use in lust spells and as a good luck travel spell.

Dogwood: Some believe Jesus was crucified on a dogwood cross. It is associated with comfort, happiness, ancestor work, banishment spells, fertility, lust, love, and will protect your secrets. If you need to protect anything written down, use the oil and the flowers, and it will ward off any prying eyes. The sap of the dogwood is thought to grant wishes, and carrying a piece on your person will ward off rabid dogs. As the name implies, dogwood is as loyal as a dog! It will help you determine which things you should exclude from your life and grant you protection from those things. Plant it around your home for protection. My grandfather planted three dogwoods around his home. Clearly, he understood the power of three. He even brought sticks from all three when he moved.

Catnip: If you want to have a psychic bond with your cat, give her a bit of catnip (it will also give your kitty a nice buzz). Combined with rose petals, catnip makes a powerful love sachet. Hold it for a while in your hand until it warms up, and then hold hands with a friend to tighten your bond. Keep the catnip you had in your hand in a safe place. Hang it over your door or grow it near your home, and it will attract great luck and good spirits. It is also used to enhance happiness and beauty spells. Boxers have been known to chew catnip before a match for increased aggressiveness and good luck.

Crystals: Ocean Jasper, Azurite, Citrine, Lapis Lazuli, Chrysoprase, and Amazonite

Earth Event: Spring equinox: Aries

Date: March 20-23

Occasion: Spring cleaning, planting seeds

BELTANE

Beltane symbolizes the full exhilaration of spring. With winter months past, nature comes alive with warmer air and vibrant shades of green bursting free. The skies are full of singing birds, and spring flowers are blooming. It is a time of renewal and passion as the Goddess is impregnated with new life. Bonfires celebrate Beltane, and the maypole is dressed with ribbons as people, young and old, dance around it. For some covens, witches celebrate coupling, or the "great rite." Altars and other sacred places are decorated with branches and spring flowers and the hair of worshipers with wreaths of flowers.

Holiday: May Day

Herbs:

Dill: Powered by magic, dill helps with romance, protection, prosperity, and more. Whip yourself up a wonderful love potion along with creating a delicious fish dinner, and romance is in the air. Use dill leaves in a ritual bath to attract romance or ward off bad dreams by hanging a sprig of dill over your bed. Wear dill on your person and keep hateful, jealous, and hurtful people out of your location. Sniff the aromatics of dill to help you through emotionally difficult times. Create a powder out of your dill and dust your purse or wallet for good luck with money. Infuse it into a cool glass of lemonade for a love potion.

Lemon balm: This beautifully aromatic citrus-scented herb added to your spellwork is truly magic. Use it for success spells and carry it on you to attract romance, relieve anxiety, and bring calmness and balance to your life. I frequently love to drink lemon balm tea to relax and calm my thoughts, and ready myself for a good night's sleep. Use it for a night of lust and romance as an aphrodisiac to increase your and your lover's desire to have intercourse. Since ancient times, sorcerers have used it as a love mixture for couples whose relationship lacks enthusiasm and romance. Use it in a love spell to draw the one you are attracted to, or float it in a glass of wine and drink it as a love potion. It has been said that lemon balm's powers are so strong that it would help someone recover from a sword slashing!

Coltsfoot: The yellow flowers of the Coltsfoot plant only open on sunny days. Its appearance is similar to a dandelion, and it belongs to the same family as the sunflower. It is one of the first plants to flower in the springtime, sometimes as early as February. It's the perfect herb for springtime rituals welcoming the return of Imbolc, Ostara, and Beltane, depending on when they blossom that particular year. Use their long stems to weave into wreaths and place them on your door for healing, money, love, and tranquility to blanket your home.

Crystals: Malachite, Magnetite, Moss Agate, Garnet, Carnelian, and Tiger's Eye

Earth Event: Taurus

Date: April 30-May 1

Occasion: Fertility, Fire celebration; Couples dance around the fire

LITHA

Midsummer and the shortest night and longest day of the year is Litha. The Sun God is at the peak of his virility, and the Goddess is pregnant, symbolizing the solar year's life-giving powers. When the Earth is engulfed with fulfillment and fertility, it is time for celebrations of joy, achievements, and expansiveness. It is a tradition to light a bonfire on Midsummer's Eve and stay up all night to watch and welcome the rising sun. The bonfires symbolize the sun's reflection at its peak strength. Oak is the chosen wood, and aromatic herbs are tossed into the fire.

Witches dance around the bonfires, leaping through them. Torches set ablaze are carried around the fields and houses in a sun-wise direction. Coals from the bonfires are littered about the fields, magically ensuring a good harvest. From here on, the nights grow longer and the days shorter, and we are taken back into the dark, completing the Wheel of the Year.

Holiday: Midsummer

Herbs:

Chicory: Known as a substitution for coffee, chicory has a rich history dating back thousands of years, where it was grown along the banks of the Nile River in Egypt. Among its magical properties are strength, removing curses, unlocking doors, divination, invisibility, obstacle removal, and good luck. The ancient Egyptians used chicory for invulnerability and to bring success. If it is pressed up against a lock, the lock will open. It was once thought to make you invisible. Using chicory oil to anoint your body will grant you favors and attract good people. While it is believed to remove curses, it is commonly used to cast a curse. When carried on your person, chicory promotes a lack of wastefulness (frugality), and when burned as an incense, it will purify and cleanse your sacred items.

Chickweed: This marvelous herb grows in groups, ever reminding us how to survive and live in balance with others and ourselves. Once when I came across a patch of chickweed, I noticed that within the group of herbs, each one had plenty of room to grow while still sitting comfortably and in close contact with the rest of the patch. It goes to show you that chickweed promotes structure and individuality within the bounds of a balanced group. With chickweed in your realm, you may want to closely examine the space you provide to others as well as your own space. Chickweed reminds us to move on if the qualities we need for a good life are not present. Chickweed teaches us not to "judge a book by its cover" and to look beyond the surface and into the people we want to grow a relationship with and to be picky as well.

Mistletoe: Mistletoe has always been thought of as magical. Two people kissing under the mistletoe promotes everlasting happiness. Carrying mistletoe on your person will bring you fertility, good luck, and protection. It has always been considered a magical, good luck plant. Lovers who kiss beneath it will have lasting happiness, and carrying a sprig on your person will ensure good luck, protection, and fertility. Hanging it in the home was supposed to protect from disease, lightning, werewolves, and having your children switched with faerie changelings.

Crystals: Citrine, Ruby, Carnelian, Garnet, Sunstone, and Tigers Eye

Earth Event: Summer solstice: Gemini

Date: June 20-22

Occasion: Gratitude for life and light; honors the Sun God

LUGHNASADH

Modern day witches celebrate the first harvest of the year as a Lughnasadh festival. Lughnasadh, also known as Lammas, acquired its name from the Old English term for "loaf mass." It originated from celebrations in early English harvest times, where loaves of bread were blessed as sacred. Many polytheists and pagans celebrate Lughnasadh by singing songs, playing games, and feasting on bread and baking cakes. At Lughnasadh, the fields of corn are being harvested, and for some, this is considered the true essence of the festival. The lore is that John Barleycorn, the character who on Beltane laid with the Lady in the woods, has now become old and stands bearded and bent over with a crooked cane. He gazes at the sun and has now turned from green to gold, and he knows it is time. His sacrifice is honored at Lughnasadh and will feed all of the people.

Holiday: First Harvest

Herbs:

Elderberry: Vibrant, juicy, wise, and protective, elderberry is encoded with celestial divinity and the ancient wisdom (Gnosis) of self-care. Since ancient times, this herb has been used for healing to treat ailments ranging from skin irritations to colds and flu to bruises and sprains. It is known in some cultures as the Holy Tree and is cherished for its magical properties and correspondence to the cycle of life, death, and rebirth. I use it in my protection, healing, and love spells.

Goldenrod: Wearing a goldenrod flower shows you on the next day your one true love. Grow around your home for prosperity. Washing a child in a goldenrod spiritual bath ensures a pleasant disposition and a good sense of humor when they are grown. Serve it in a tea to seal the emotions of your lover. If you have lost something, hold a stalk of goldenrod flowers in your hand, and it will point you in the direction of your lost item. Carry it in your purse or wallet for good fortune. As the main source of nectar, goldenrod offers a seasonal snack for butterflies, moths, bees, flies, beetles, wasps, and many more insect and animal kingdom residents. The larvae of many insect species feast on the leaves of the goldenrod. It encourages us to bring forth offerings and stand tall against adversity, mistruths, and old stories.

Sunflower: Nothing symbolizes the innate wisdom given by the Great Sun like the sunflower. Beautiful, fleeting, and bold, sunflowers show off their vibrancy and their magical empowerment. The striking resemblance of a lion's mane to the sunflower's head provides the perfect essence for spells about courage. Grab some sunflowers while they are in season to dispel shyness, and stimulate you into taking bold steps towards times of uncertainty. Bring this flower to your solar rituals for fertility spells and friendship blessings. Place a bouquet of sunflowers in any room where someone is ill, and the negative energy will be chased away. Because of their rewarding solar vibes, they are the perfect spiritual "disinfectant."

Crystals: Clear Quartz, Pink Quartz, Amber, Jasper, and Sunstone

Earth Event: Halfway between the summer solstice and autumn equinox: Leo

Occasion: Symbolic gifts of the first fruits as offerings to a deity; honoring hard work that pays off

MABON

Mabon is named after the Welsh God. He is the son of Mother Earth Modron and the Child of Light. This is another example of the journey of perfect balance through the Wheel of the Year. Day and night are equal once again - masculine, feminine, outer and inner, all in balance. At this point, the year is beginning to wane, and from here on out, darkness defeats the light. The natural cycle of the world is heading towards completion. The power of the sun is waning, and the days are shorter and cooler. The tree's sap returns to its roots, and the summer green changes to the fire of autumn.

Holiday: Thanksgiving

Herbs:

Yarrow: Revered for its physical, spiritual, and magical properties, yarrow has a plethora of medicinal benefits. It is an ancient herb named after the great legendary hero Achilles. It is used for love, healing, and courage spells. It was written that Achilles used yarrow to soothe the muscles and for healing other injuries on the battlefield. I use it to clean my skin, and I love it. If you are ever feeling a bit melancholic, call upon the magic of yarrow to heal your mind, spirit, and body when it seems to be unmovable. Let it ground you in times of strife and help you to renew your foundation. Yarrow will ground you without weighing you down and will give you discernment and clarity.

Rue: From the stealthy evergreen shrub with its yellow blossoms and woody stems arising during the summertime, rue is an herb of purification, balance, and protection. According to the Bible, it was given as a tithe, and in the days of antiquity, this herb was quite popular in Roman cuisine, even though it has a bitter taste. Burn it as an incense to promote clarity and reduce anxiety. Often utilized in health and protection spells, rue also comes in handy for breaking curses and hexes. It was considered the witches' herb during the middle ages. From my research, I have learned that witches seem not to like the smell of rue, but neither do disease-carrying rats! It was used in ancient times by wise people in potions against other witches. I read that Michelangelo and Leonardo DaVinci used rue in small amounts to enhance their creativity. The one thing I know it is good for is insect repellent. WARNING: NOT FOR HUMAN CONSUMPTION!

Crystals: Tiger's Eye, Clear Quartz, Citrine, Ruby, Topaz, and Moss Agate

Earth Event: Autumnal equinox: Virgo

Date: September 20-23

Occasion: Time for resting after the hard work of the harvest; a time to reap what was sown; time for finishing up projects

4

ESSENTIAL HERBS

Nutmeg does more than make fantastic eggnog, and cayenne pepper does more than put heat into your chili! The spices you have in your kitchen pantry are brimming with magical properties just waiting for you to tap into! Not only will this list of commonly used spices and herbs add power to your spells, but it will also allow you to connect your spiritual and magical practices together and use them both in your daily life. The following are the 31 most commonly used herbs in magic:

ALLSPICE

Allspice was used to embalm the dead by the ancient Mayans and to cure meat by the Arawak. South Americans also used it to add flavor to chocolate. Allspice got its name in English because of its aromatic qualities of multiple spices, such as cloves, cinnamon, pepper, juniper berries, and nutmeg. Allspice

THE HERB MAGIC SPELL BOOK | 41

has been known to soothe a toothache, act as a breath freshener, and aid digestion. It is useful to many healing spells.

Latin Name: P. dioica

Folk Names: Pimenta, Jamaican Pepper

Element: Fire

Magical Uses: Money, positivity, luck, uplifting mood, increases energy, and determination

BASIL

Starting in India over 5000 years ago, basil has become a staple herb in magical, medicinal, and culinary practices. The word basil means "fragrant" and stems from the Greek word meaning "King," associated with royalty and wealth. But, it is more associated with romance and love than it is royalty and wealth. The correspondence between love and basil is so powerful that in the past, men wore basil in their hats when preparing to court a woman. Offer a sprig of basil to someone to whom you are attracted to divine a future lover. Sprinkle some basil over your lover's heart to ensure that they will remain faithful.

Latin Name: Ocimum spp.

Folk Names: King of herbs, Witches herb

Element: Fire

Magical Uses: Love spells, protection rituals and spells, prosperity spells, hedge riding (astral travel), purification, peace, and banishment

BAY LEAVES

(DON'T CONSUME IF PREGNANT)

The aromatic bay leaves of the laurel have a deep history in mythology and folklore. Mentioned in Homer's Odyssey and the Bible, bay leaves are most commonly known for their culinary properties but also for their attendance in wreaths given to triumphant Olympic athletes. However, in ancient mythology, Daphne was a nymph who was transformed into a laurel tree to protect her virginity from the hot pursuit of Apollo. To the ancient Romans, the bay leaf symbolized glory and was viewed as protection against thunder, lightning, evil, and the plague. Roman soldiers cleaned the blood off of their weapons with bay leaves. In ancient Elizabethan times, it was believed disaster would follow the death of a laurel tree.

Latin Name: Laurus nobilis

Folk Names: Bay, Bay Laurel, Bay Tree, Daphne, Grecian Laurel, Laurel, Laurel Común, Laurier d'Apollon, Laurier Noble, Laurier-Sauce, Laurier Vrai, Mediterranean Bay, Noble Laurel, Roman Laurel, and True Bay

Element: Fire

Magical Uses: Exorcism, banishing, fidelity, empowerment, luck, wealth, psychic development, and wishing

BLACK PEPPER

Black pepper is earthy, spicy, and amazingly grounding. It has an incredible ability to create endurance and strength to express yourself freely. Grown in Southern India, pepper has been used in magic for more than 2000 years. It is considered in Asian cultures to be a powerful herb thought to support healthy aging, detoxify the liver, and aid in digestion and circulation. As the story goes, during the 5th century, Attila the Hun demanded 4,000 pounds of black pepper be paid in ransom for the city of Rome. It was heavily used in the Middle Ages and by the ancient Romans and became a staple of fine cuisine.

Latin Name: Piper nigrum

Folk Names: Benin pepper, Uziza seeds, Ashanti pepper, and False Cubeb

Element: Fire

Magical Uses: Protection, exorcism, jealousy, negativity, strength, confidence, and gossip

CAYENNE

Cayenne peppers have a history spanning over 8000 years and started out as a ritualistic and decorative item, later finding their way into the culinary world and the world of medicine. I read an article that said they found seeds on the grounds of cave dwellings of the ancient primitive peoples in Mexico[1]. In the 1500s, cayenne was valued in trade in areas where it did not grow, and some of the ancient Indians used it as offerings to their gods. They were also used in South America in smoke form, as a weapon against invading troops. Cayenne is usually used in powder form for spicy dishes. Some pickle them, and some eat them whole! These peppers are commonly harvested in Mexico, India, East Africa, and the U.S. They are named after the cayenne region of French Guiana. The Tupi Indians gave cayenne its name. It has many beneficial health attributes, especially for the cardiovascular system. It lowers your cholesterol and your triglyceride levels. It has been used for centuries and is also sold as an herbal supplement. Cayenne is also known as "the healing spice." Please do not use cayenne in equal amounts to paprika, not that you don't know better, but just in case.

Latin Name: Capsicum annuum

Folk Names: Africa peppers, Bird pepper, Zanzibar pepper, Goat's pepper, Spanish pepper, and Cockspur pepper

Element: Fire

Magical Uses: Spiritual connection, strengthens the magical powers of other herbs, purification of water and home, rids the home of negative energy, removes obstacles, and helps you reach your goals

CINNAMON

Cinnamon dates back to 3000 B.C. in documented Chinese writings and is still known today in Cantonese as kwai. When used as an incense, cinnamon can create elevated spiritual vibrations and aid in attracting positive energies such as money, healing, and protection from evil. Sprinkle some around your home to protect and purify it. Add a bit of cinnamon to your plant water, and they will be purified of all negativity. Cinnamon has been known to have antiviral, bactericidal, and antifungal properties. It has been used medicinally to prevent the spread of certain types of bacteria and viruses. During medieval times, healers or doctors used cinnamon medicinally to treat sore throats, coughing, and hoarseness. Most interestingly, Roman Emperor Nero, out of remorse for murdering his wife, ordered a year's supply of cinnamon be burnt in her honor.[2]

Latin Name: Cinnamomum verum

Folk Names: Kwai, Sweet Wood, and Ceylon

Element: Fire

Magical Uses: Esotericism, white magic, healing, protection, love, success, power, and sexual desire

CLOVES

In 200 BC, convoys carried cloves from Java to the court of the Han dynasty in China. Believe it or not, it was used as a breath freshener. There were even clove battles in the 17th century, where the Dutch decimated cloves on all of the Spice Islands to keep the prices high by creating scarcity - the whole "supply and demand" concept. Cloves were an important herb in the early days of the spice trade. They are indigenous to the Spice Islands of Indonesia. Their aroma is hot and strong in taste but they are used to flavor meats and bakery items. In the U.S. and Europe, it is known as the holiday spice in such fare as mincemeat, fruitcake, and wassail.

Latin Name: Syzygium aromaticum

Folk Names: Mykhet, Carenfil

Element: Fire

Magical Uses: Enhances spiritual vibrations, purification, prosperity, wards off negative and hostile forces, clarity, empathy, healing, and memory

CUMIN

Cumin has been chronicled since the dawn of written history and has been popular for just as long. For centuries it has been a staple in love spells. One very interesting fact about cumin is that it is the only word in the English language that can be traced back to the first language ever written, Sumerian ("Gamun"), 4000 years ago. Another amazing fact about cumin is that it is an ingredient in the oldest recipe in human history (1750 BC) on the Mesopotamian tablets. It was placed as an offering at the tombs of ancient Egyptian pharaohs.

Latin Name: Cuminum Cyminum

Folk Names: Cumino, Cumino Aigro, Kamûnu

Element: Fire

Magical Uses: Fidelity, repels evil, love, peace, exorcism, passion, aphrodisiac, and protection against thieves

CURRY

There are many magic herbs grown on Indian soil. A close friend of mine grew up in India, and she told me that curry is not just an herb; it is a sentiment. She grew up savoring many different curry dishes as a staple meal for years. She and I shared a love for the distinct flavor of these savory and spicy curries that seem to dance on our taste buds. Needless to say, I use curry in many of my spells. It is important to use actual curry in your spells and not a spice blend, because all spices have their own magical properties. Curry leaves are one of the many magic herbs that are found and grown on Indian soil.

Latin Name: Initam volebant

Folk Names: Krishi Jagran, Kadi Patta

Element: Fire

Magical Uses: Protection, burn at nightfall to ward off evil energies

DANDELION ROOT

Every spring, I look forward to seeing my yard suddenly blanketed with the bright and sunny yellow faces of the dandelions. Some people I know spend loads of money trying to eradicate these magical little flowers. The truth is that dandelions have a rich and long history in folklore, both from a medicinal and a magical perspective. Do you remember when you were a kid, and you would make a wish and blow on a dandelion, and when you did, the little seeds would carry your wish in the wind to fruition? Even today, I hold a dandelion under my chin to see if it reflects yellow. If it does, I know I am coming into some money! This magic dates back to before medieval times.

Latin Name: Taraxacum

Folk Names: Blowball, Cankerwort, Lion's Tooth, Priest's Crown, Puffball, Swine's Snout, White Endive, and Wild Endive

Element: Air

Magical Uses: Growth, transformation, ridding yourself of a bad habit, overcoming adversity, wish granting, psychic abilities, dreams coming true, and second sight

DILL

Dill's rich history dates back to 3000 BC, as well as the Middle Ages where it was known to have the power to destroy evil and break any evil spells cast against someone by a witch. It is native to the eastern Mediterranean region and western Asia. It was documented in ancient Egyptian medical works thousands of years before Christ. Just the word dill brings to your mind pickles! Believe it or not, Americans eat more than 2 ½ billion pounds each year! Dill has been a staple herb used widely in Nordic countries to flavor seafood.

Latin Name: Anethum graveolens

Folk Names: Aneto, Aneton, Dill Weed, Dill Seed, Dilly, and Garden Dill

Element: Fire

Magical Uses: Lust, protection, money, luck, love, warding off dark forces, blessing your house, keeping you informed about the difference between superstition and magic, and attraction

DOGWOOD

Cultivated first in 1730, the dogwood tree is native to Asia, North America, and Europe. Use of the dogwood was documented by Native Americans long before settlers came to America. The flower of the dogwood became the state flower of North Carolina in 1941 and the state tree in Missouri in 1955. The dogwood holds a profound meaning to some people based on a legendary story from 2000 years ago. Folklore has it that the dogwood felt great sympathy and anguish for the suffering of Jesus Christ, crucified on a cross made from the dogwood tree. It is said that Jesus felt the tree's sorrow and transformed it so that it could never again be used for crucifixions, and this is why the dogwood is now a shrub-like tree with twisted limbs[3].

Latin Name: Cornus

Folk Names: Boxwood, Squawbush, Budwood, Flowering Cornel, and Green Osier

Elements: Air, Water, and Fire

Magical Uses: Protection, stability, kindness, confidence, guards journals, diaries, letters, and Books of Shadows

DRAGON'S BLOOD

Off the Horn of Africa is an island that carries a tree's root with a menacing crown with vein-type branches that trickle a deep-red resin. The Dracaena cinnabari has earned its name in blood throughout history with legends of magic and dragons. By carefully cutting small incisions, locals collect the blood-colored resin and let it dry. Dating back to 17th century Europe, dragon's blood was valued as a cure-all. Medical practitioners prescribed dragon's blood for serious health conditions. We know now that it has anti-inflammatory and antimicrobial properties. It was also used in ancient times as a breath freshener and for magic in love potions.

Latin Name: Dracaena cinnabari

Folk Names: Blood, Blume, Calamus Draco, Dragon's Blood Palm

Element: Fire

Magical Uses: Protection, spell potency, banishing, preventing impotence, protects your business, luck, purification, and magical ink

ECHINACEA

Native to North America, Echinacea is known by many different Native American tribes. It is called "elk root" by the Ute, a Western Indian tribe. They hold the belief that if an elk is injured, it seeks out the Echinacea as a medication. It has been a traditional healing herb used by many tribes from the Midwest to the Great Plains to treat burns, swelling, and pain. It is also known as Coneflower and has been part of Sun Dance rituals throughout Native American history. The Navajo consider it sacred and chew it while they dance during ceremonial rituals.

Latin Name: Echinacea purpurea

Folk Names: Purple Coneflower, Coneflower, Black Sampson, Rudbeckia

Element: Earth

Magical Uses: Money, offerings, protection, power, exorcism, added strength for spells and charms, fertility, healing, clairvoyant and psychic abilities

ELDER

In Scandinavian and English folklore, Hyldemoer or Sambucus or "Elder Mother" was believed to inhabit the Sambucus or Elder Tree. Hyldemoer is the nymph or goddess of vegetation, life, and death and has the dual power to harm or protect. Legend has it that one should ask permission of the Elder to use part of her tree for its magical and protective qualities or be prepared to be cursed. One method for asking the Elder Mother for her permission is to give offerings to her and speak aloud, "Elder Mother, may I have your wood, and I will give you mine when I become a tree?" NOT FOR HUMAN CONSUMPTION.

Latin Name: Sambucus

Folk Names: Tree of Doom, Pipe Tree, Witch's Tree, Old Lady, Devil's Eye

Element: Earth

Magical Uses: Wisdom, home and business blessings, protection, death and dying transportation to the Otherworld, dream pillows

EUCALYPTUS

The Eucalyptus is native to Australia and stems from the Greek words "eu" and "kalyptos," meaning beautiful hat, because the pistils and stamens together look like a hat. Eucalyptus is the Aboriginals' holy tree. It symbolizes, for them, the division between the Earth and Heaven, or the Underworld. Its leaves, when burned, ward off negative energy.

Latin Name: Eucalyptus globulus

Folk Names: Blue Gum, Curly Mallee, River Red Gum, Mottlecah, Maiden's Gum, Fever Tree, Stringy Bark Tree

Element: Air

Magical Uses: Protection, healing, purification, reconcile relationships, health and wellness, clarity, raises positive vibrations, repels enemies, overcome jealousy, and ward off evil

EVENING PRIMROSE

Considered by some to be a weed and others a wildflower, Evening Primrose comes in colors of yellow, purple, pink, and white with lance-shaped leaves that spiral, beginning on the ground and moving up and around the stem, into a cup-shaped flower. It only blooms at night, hence the name Evening Primrose, and closes the next day before the noon hour. Make sure to pick your starter plants based on their scientific name, because not all species have this trait.

Latin Name: Oenothera

Folk Names: Fever Plant, Field Primrose, King's Cureall, Night Willow-herb, Scabish, Scurvish

Element: Water

Magical Uses: Altar decorations, ritual baths, desirability, beauty, luck for a new job, hunting, and goal success.

FENNEL SEED

Ancient folklore called the fennel plant the snake herb, as it is believed that snakes sharpen their eyesight by rubbing against it. The Puritans would chew fennel seeds at church, giving them the name "meeting seeds." It has a part in European history, as it has grown wildly around the Mediterranean basin for millennia. The Old English word for fennel is "hay."

Latin Name: Foeniculum vulgare

Folk Names: Snake herb, Large fennel, Sweet fennel, Wild fennel, Finocchio, Carosella, Florence fennel, and Fennel seed

Element: Air

Magical Uses: Sexual virility, protection, purification, healing, courage, vitality, increase the length of incarnation, and ward off evil

FEVERFEW

Feverfew grows, albeit short-lived, in Greece, Egypt, Australia, and North America. It was used in Ancient Egypt and Greece by medicine practitioners for ailments such as inflammation, pain management, and menstrual cramps. Folklore says you can protect your family from disease by planting feverfew flowers by the door of your house. It was used in medieval times during plagues to ward off illness. It is documented that rats carrying the plague hated the smell and taste of feverfew, so they avoided eating it. Because of its connection to curing pains and aches, it is also known by some to cure feelings of rejection in love and heart-sickness. Folklore also has it that feverfew protects against elf shot, which was thought to be a sudden stabbing pain caused by the arrow shot by an invisible elf. Today this pain is thought of as a charlie horse or even arthritis.

Latin Name: Tanacetum parthenium

Folk Names: Featherfew, Rainfarn, Wild Quinine, Feather-foil, Prairie Dock, Missouri Snakeroot, Flirtwort, Parthenium, Febrifuge, Devil Daisy, Bachelor's Button, Maid's Weed, Midsummer Daisy, Nosebleed, Vetter-voo, Wild Chamomile, or Matricaria.

Element: Water

Magical Uses: Protection when traveling and against accidents, health and wellness, and spirituality

FIG

Fig trees are featured in origin stories around the world. The best-known origin story is that the leaves of the fig tree clothed Adam and Eve. Another story about the great fig is that it provided shelter for a she-wolf whom a baby boy suckled and who later went on to found Rome. Yet another story of the great fig tree is that its leaves created the tongues of the first people, as well as provided their food and shelter.

Latin Name: Ficus carica

Folk Names: Common fig

Element: Fire

Magical Uses: Travel, answering questions (if its leaves dry slowly, it's a "yes," otherwise, it's a "no,"), divination, love, and fertility

FLAXSEED

Latin Name: Linum usitatissimum

Folk Name: Linseed

Element: Water

Magical Uses: Healing, money, protection when mixed with red pepper, divination, future telling, and keeps away poverty

FRANKINCENSE

One of the oldest known magical resins is that of frankincense. It has been an item of trade in parts of the Arab world and Africa for more than 5000 years. It is mentioned in the book of Matthew as a gift given by the Three Wise Men after the birth of Jesus Christ. Frankincense is also mentioned many times in the Talmud and the Old Testament. It has been a staple in many Jewish and Christian rituals and ceremonies.

Latin Name: Boswellia sacra

Folk Names: Frankincense Tears and Olibanum

Element: Water

Magical Uses: Consecration, protection, success, meditation, self-control, manifestation, brings success, offering at Yule, Beltane, and Lammas, and elevated topaz power

FUMITORY

Fumitory is believed to be a protective herb since ancient times. It is documented as far back as the Stone Age, 9000 BC. It can slowly grow at almost freezing temperatures, so it was one of the first emerging weeds. It fertilizes itself and can take over gardens and crops. Because it grows in lighter types of soil, it has earned the name of "beggary." It was thought to protect against evil spirits and witchcraft. NOT FOR HUMAN CONSUMPTION.

Latin Name: Fumaria officinalis

Folk Name: Earth Smoke, Drug fumitory, Hedge fumitory, Beggary, and Wax Dolls

Element: Fire

Magical Uses: Consecrating tools for rituals, purification, use at Samhain, new home blessings, money draw, protect your property, and attract love spells

GINSENG

For thousands of years, ginseng has been thought to be a necessity for life in China. This strong cultural belief is that it slows the aging process, prevents illness, and stimulates sexual arousal. Ginseng's history dates back to before the Declaration of Independence in America. Native Americans used ginseng for spiritual rituals, and the medicine man prescribed it for digestive health and to treat fevers. It has also been used worldwide as an aphrodisiac.

Latin Name: Panax ginseng

Folk Names: Sang, Wonder of the World Root

Element: Fire

Magical Uses: Lust, beauty, love, money, wishes, healing, protection, sexual potency, health and wellness

HAWTHORN

The tree most likely to be protected or inhabited by the Wee Folk is the mighty hawthorn tree. Most of the lone bushes or isolated hawthorn trees in Ireland are said to house fairies. You can't hurt a hawthorn tree without incurring the wrath, often deadly, of the faeries. The Faery Queen next to her hawthorn is believed to represent a pre-Christian archetype. I always picture myself worshiping the Faery Queen as a goddess during a ritual in a sacred hawthorn grove! It is also known as the May tree because it blossoms during May.

Latin Name: Crataegus

Folk Names: Haw, May bush, May tree, Mayblossom, Mayflower, Quickset, Thorn-apple tree, Whitethorn, Bread and Cheese tree, Quick, Gazels, Ladies' Meat

Element: Fire

Magical Uses: Faeries, chastity, fertility, fishing, happiness, protection against lightning, ghost repellent, wards off evil spirits, removes negativity, profession, employment, and celibacy

HYACINTH

Hyacinth was named after the Greek hero, Hyakinthos, who Apollo beloved, and for this reason, it is considered the protection herb of homosexual men. According to Greek mythology, Hyakinthos gave hyacinth the divine attributes known to the plant. It was believed the herb was created from Hyakinthos' spilled blood when he was killed by Zeypherus, the North Wind God, because of his jealousy for Apollo's love for him. In Apollo's grief, he wouldn't let Hades take Hyakinthos to the Underworld, so he resurrected him as the hyacinth plant.

Latin Name: Hyacinthus

Folk Names: English Bluebells, Wood hyacinth, Endymion, or Nodding Squill

Element: Fire

Magical Uses: Love, money, homosexuality, dreams, peaceful sleep, eases the pain of childbirth, and good fortune

JUNIPER

Juniper has been used throughout history as an herb to ward off disease. It has been tied to magical practices for the workings of fire and for its herbal wisdom. Traditionally, magicians have used juniper in spells to retrieve stolen items. Its history dates back to ancient times, where its documented use in rites of purification and to drive away evil spirits is listed in the Key of Solomon, a 14th century Book of Spells.

Latin Name: Juniperus

Folk Names: Juniper berries, Ginepro, Enebro, Wachholder, Eastern Red Cedar, Red juniper, Baton Rouge, Pencil cedar, and Savin

Element: Fire

Magical Uses: Potency, attract love, safeguard against thievery, prosperity, healthy energies, banishing harmful things toward good health, attract positivity, healthy energies

MANDRAKE

The ancient Greeks used mandrake as an aphrodisiac, and it was known as the "love-apple of the ancient peoples." The ancient Hebrews believed mandrake induced conception. The roots of the mandrake are said to look weirdly like a human body, and legend says it reveals itself in female and male forms. One legend holds that mandrake springs from the blood, semen, and fat of a hanged man and that if you pull it from the ground, it lets out a blood-curdling scream, projecting pain and death to anyone within earshot. I have been near many mandrakes. Thank heavens I never tried to pull one out of the ground! NOT FOR HUMAN CONSUMPTION.

Latin Name: Mandragora officinarum

Folk Names: Mandragora, Satan's Apple, Manroot, Circeium, Gallows, Herb of Circe, Mandragora, Raccoon Berry, Ladykins, Womandrake, Sorcerer's Root, Wild Lemon

Element: Fire

Magical Uses: Protection, prosperity, fertility, exorcising evil, attracting love, and preserving health

PATCHOULI

Patchouli was a favorite among the hippie movement of the 1960s and 1970s. The word patchouli comes from the Hindi word for "scent." Its history spans thousands of years. It is documented that King Tut had patchouli oil buried with him in his tomb. Europeans historically traded patchouli for gold, and it has been the standard of many fabrics such as silk to act as a protectant against insects.

Latin Name: Pogostemon cablin

Folk Names: Patchouly, Pucha Pot

Element: Earth

Magical Uses: Fertility, grounding, drawing money, love, spiritual bathing, business growth, return from other realms to the spiritual world

SAFFRON

The origin of saffron is in Asia Minor, where the trade industry used the stems to dye fabrics imported from Phoenicians. It was then spread by the Arabs in their conquests against India and Spain. Already precious to the Romans, saffron was described by the famous poet Ovid in the 1st century. Towards the latter part of the 1300s, during the Spanish inquisition, saffron cultivation began, and there started its production.

Latin Name: Crocus sativus

Folk Names: Kum Kuma, Zaffran, Kesar, Autumn Crocus, Spanish saffron, Dyer's saffron, Thistle saffron, Bastard saffron, American saffron, and Parrot's Corn

Element: Water

Magical Uses: Happiness, strength, healing, love spells, lust, raising the power of wind, increasing psychic awareness, controlling the weather, and aphrodisiac

VALERIAN

The word valerian comes from the Latin word "valere," meaning to be healthy and strong. In this case, "strong" may mean its powerful healing properties or may mean "strong" in odor. The ancient Greeks referred to this herb as "Phu" as in "Phew!" Throughout history, it has been believed that valerian has the ability to turn anything bad into something good.

Latin Name: Valeriana officinalis

Folk Names: All-Heal, Garden Heliotrope, Graveyard Dust, Phu, Setwell, Vandal Root

Element: Water

Magical Uses: Protection, harmony, substitution for graveyard dirt (as long as all involved agree), repairs relationships, dream magic, purification, calmness, reconciliation, and settles arguments

5

GATHERING HERBS IN NATURE

Of all of the wondrous things to do in this world, one of the most spiritual and enjoyable activities I do is gather herbs in nature. Learning about them, picking my own delicious berries, and finding gems on the land after I just looked them up online is monumentally rewarding. I use them in teas, cleansing bundles, culinary creations, to charge my crystals, spiritual baths, my spells, and so much more! Some gardeners have their own unique take on handling herbs. Rather than dismissing them as maddening or mundane, I have chosen to embrace wild herbs with all of their magic, deliciousness, and enchantment. Some call it "foraging." I prefer "wildcrafting." Either way, collecting your own herbs is one of the most empowering and spiritual practices one can undertake. It means taking the time and putting in the effort to educate yourself about the plants' virtues, properties, and benefits. The process of learning how to identify herbs and their habitat, how to cultivate them in your garden, and how to use them in magic means you have chosen a life of self-care and oneness with the Elements.

Before we get started, it is essential to mention that self-care and self-treatment are two different things. There are always cases when it is advised to seek a medical professional, so remember while holistic forms of healing are very helpful, they do not take the place of conventional medicine when necessary. Besides, chances are, your doctor might prescribe a complementary treatment with herbs anyway. That being said, it is also important to know how to gather your herbs in a way that does not harm the plant populations themselves or needlessly take the life of a plant.

Rule #1: Ensure the herb you are gathering is the herb you think it is.

Rule #2: NEVER ingest an herb you have not identified with certainty. That means knowing what it looks like and which herbs look like the one you are looking for.

Two of my buddies were wildcrafting one day and thought they would chew on the roots of a cattail they picked from the edge of the pond near my house. I wasn't with them because I was making salads so we could add their wonderful finds. Before I even finished preparing lunch, the two of them were in the bathroom vomiting and pooping. The herb they decided to chew on was an iris, not a cattail! Cattail is edible, and iris is not! So be very careful you identify what you forage before you put anything in your mouth. This was a mild case of poisonous look-alikes, but it could have been much more serious or even deadly with other herb imposters.

If you are picking up your basket for wildcrafting for the first time, make it a ritual because this is truly a special moment. Getting to know your locally-grown herbs and then bringing them home to your apothecary and kitchen will be one of the most spiritual life experiences you have ever had. When I first started wildcrafting, I focused on a specific range of generous, plentiful, and beneficial herbs, so I looked to the common flora, wild weeds, and those that quite frankly were invasive. I strongly suggest you do the same. These particulars also happen to be some of the most nutrient-dense and medicinal allies of wild foods. Remember, we also want to practice sustainability by honoring Mother Earth. Many of these feral plants are my main choices because they are the most sustainable wild food options out there. Plus, they are not difficult to find and become friends with. Believe me, just connecting to these wonderful botanicals is spellwork at its finest.

Tools You Need

I had no idea what tools I needed when I first started. I only brought a basket, which seems funny now. All wildcrafters have a set of sacred tools. Plus, you can also use them for your gardening.

1. Sunscreen
2. Hat

3. Gardening gloves

4. Books to identify plants (I didn't think of these the first time I went collecting and then realized I didn't know what anything was!)

5. Pruners are the tool you will use most often when gathering and processing your wild herbs. They will snip their way right through twigs, roots, small branches, and herbaceous stems. I use them so often that I keep them in a holster on a leather belt so I can reach down to my hip when I need them.

6. Weeding knife, or Japanese garden knife called a hori-hori: having a sturdy knife is an excellent wildcrafting tool and a great weeding instrument. I use mine to dig small roots from the earth and break up soil or pry up rocks. They also come in handy for transplanting roots. I keep mine in my leather holster. I suggest getting tools with wooden handles because they are sturdier than plastic. If you tend to lose things, get tools with orange or red handles so they will be easier to find.

7. Digging fork: This is the best tool for digging up roots. The fork tines are effective in loosening soil and lifting roots from the ground. I also use mine to weed my garden and harvest roots I use in my spells.

8. Gathering baskets: I love picking my basket for the day. They come in handy for gathering and drying herbs, and they are beautiful to look at. It's helpful to have an assortment on hand. You can typically find

used baskets in thrift stores. Look for a few with an open weave that are broad and flattish (helpful for increasing ventilation when drying loose herbs). The bottom line is to enjoy your baskets.

9. Pruning saw: This tool is good for cutting small branches and gathering medicinal barks from wild cherry and birch trees.

10. Bags, labels, and markers: Don't keep your herbs in plastic bags unless you refrigerate them. Label them with different color markers and date them.

Learn your Latin names: Don't always depend on common names because they can apply to different plants, and some edible plants share the same common names as toxic plants. Hemlock is a good example, as poisonous hemlock is Conium maculatum, and the edible Eastern hemlock is Tsuga canadensis. The Latin names were used to title plants because there is no chance of the language evolving or changing, since it is a dead language.

Use your senses: Lots of plants, including edibles, have look-alikes. So use your sense of smell and texture. While not always the case, many toxic plants smell awful and are unpalatable. However, don't go around tasting plants. Obviously, some, even in very small doses, are deadly.

Learn your habitats: Learn about your habitats. A plant's habitat must have enough space, water, and food. Each habitat has identifying characteristics that correspond with different types of herbs. Not every herb can live in the desert, nor in the marshlands, nor the woodlands. You won't find ramps in the marsh nor cattails on high slopes. There are many types of woodlands and forests, depending on the climate. I love to use journaling and I write down things I learn from living books or encyclopedias and diagram them with each habitat I explore.

Know your seasons: Journal how they change with each season. Learning to follow your herbs through the seasons is a way to identify changing plants. Sometimes by the time they are identifiable, they are past the point where you can use them. If you start taking notes early, such as in summertime, you will know where to find your herbs when they first sprout in the spring. If you are steadfast with your journaling, as the months and years go by, you will have created a calendar that tells you what to look forward to harvesting. Foraging in the spring is all about the cornucopia of wild greens that are nutritious and abundant. It is a traditional ritual for cleansing your spirit and your body after a long winter. Chickweed, dandelion, wintercress, daylilies, and stinging nettles are all out there for spring-picking.

Summer's herbs are full of antioxidant mushrooms, berries, and flowers. This is the season of colorful herbs and, most of all, the best time of the year for drying and preserving your herbs. You can dry them, freeze them, ferment them, make jam, or infuse them in your favorite beverage. Others can be dried and stored for your spellcrafting year-round. On the other hand, fall brings earthy, sweeter, and softer herbs to your baskets. Fall is the time for savory nuts, sun-toasted seeds, edible roots, and ripening fruits. This is the time to gather as much as you can before the months of frosty winter.

Know which parts of the plants are safe: Just because you know certain plants are edible doesn't mean all parts are edible. For example, the roots, bark, and stems of elderberries are poisonous, even though ripe, cooked elderberries are safe to consume.

Dos and Don'ts

1. No trespassing.
2. Watch your footing. Sometimes you may be tempted to scale a hill that is too steep, or you may find yourself on a slippery slope. SAFETY FIRST.
3. Watch out for poison ivy and poison oak. The first time I got poison ivy, it was like watching myself touch it in slow motion. No sooner did I see it than I knew I would soon be looking for the calamine lotion.
4. Wear boots and gloves.
5. Watch out for snakes.
6. Don't carry more than you need.
7. Express your gratitude. "Spirits of these herbs, I give thanks, from the hillsides to the banks, may you nourish and heal us, I give you all of my trust. So it is and should be."
8. Know the foraging laws in your areas. For instance, it is illegal to harvest herbs or pick flowers in a National

Park. Each public area has different rules, so check first. Even if you think you won't get caught, you don't want to give wildcrafters like me a bad name. Besides, some of the rules are to protect our ecosystem, so check your local guidelines.

9. Harvest at the most 25% of the plant to avoid overharvesting. I read that sage and ramps are becoming more scarce due to overharvesting. Learn about what herbs are rare because they may seem plentiful in your area but are diminishing overall. This is also happening because habitats are growing smaller.

10. Don't forage near busy roads. Many leaves absorb metals and lead from toxic exhaust. The toxins from the highways tend to settle in the soil. Also, make sure you check on the pesticides in the areas you are wildcrafting.

11. The same goes for foraging in any water source. Unfortunately, most water sources are polluted or are becoming polluted. Eating a plant from polluted water is the same as drinking contaminated water. You also don't want these chemicals mixed into your spells and rituals. Heavy metals do not cook away.

12. Ask permission to forage. It is the courteous thing to do if you think you may be on someone's property. I always do. The one time I didn't (because I didn't know I was on private property), the owner came up to me on a four-wheeler and told me I was trespassing. I was embarrassed and never made that mistake again.

6

GROWING YOUR OWN HERBS

As much as I enjoy growing my own vegetables, I really believe starting with an herb garden is the best choice. It doesn't take a great deal of effort to reap the benefits of being able to sense their magic all around you while at the same time doing something healthy. It's easier to grow your own herbal garden than growing vegetables or flowers. You can grow them in pots indoors, or if the soil in your yard is nutritious enough, you can grow them in your yard. There are even hydroponic kits, like the AeroGarden, for your indoor herbal garden, but I chose to learn about each species and do it myself. I grow mine in pots that I can put on my patio where they always get the morning sun. Most can handle a broad range of temperatures. Just a couple of steps in the morning, and I have fresh basil for my omelet. While they are a great addition to my eggs, I also use them in salves, teas, essential oils, and tinctures.

I first started with transplants, and then as I learned more, I used seeds. You can even have different herbs in the same pot, but you have to be careful because some, like mint, will take over. Having your own organic herbs from your garden is so self-fulfilling and benefits your health in many ways. Detoxifying and strengthening your immune system helps prevent the common cold, aids in digestion, lowers your stress levels, and so much more. Just about every morning, as soon as I get up, except during the hottest months, I step out onto my patio and pick a few leaves of basil for my breakfast. This easy and quick access to fresh organic herbs is far above anything I can get at the grocery store. By having your own herb garden, you can grow what you want for your taste and magical preferences.

Some of the medicinal or healing herbs I grow include:

- Chamomile is not only delicious but helps to relax me and promotes a good night's sleep.
- Peppermint eases nausea, provides clarity, boosts your mood, and eases digestion.
- Lavender helps improve sleep, remedy pain, lowers heart rate and blood pressure, eases hot flashes from menopause, promotes hair growth, and relieves congestion.
- Echinacea I keep around to fight off the cold season. It has many medicinal properties, including helping relieve and cure urinary tract infections.
- Oregano is loaded with antioxidants, has antifungal

and antibacterial properties, and boosts your immune system.

- Rosemary has anti-inflammatory compounds that improve your circulation, is a cognitive stimulant, enhances the quality and performance of your memory, and raises your focus and alertness.

Spending Time in a Garden is Healthy

While enjoying the improved physical health your herb garden provides, actually tending to them welcomes in their magical properties. Tending to your herbal garden provides you with the opportunity to live a more healthy and active lifestyle. Being one with Mother Nature puts you in an atmosphere of fresh air rich in vitamin D, and offers some good exercise at the same time. All of the qualities of home gardening lead to a higher quality of life, allow you time to unplug from your smart devices, and lower your stress. It is proven to be therapeutic for your mental and spiritual health. Spending time outside visiting with your herbs, watering them, singing to them, all of it is healthy for both. Working with dirt physically puts you in touch with microorganisms, minerals, and bacteria that boost your immune system. Exposing yourself to these small quantities of bacteria allows your immune system to strengthen and protect you against diseases and potential allergies later in life.

Earthing

Earthing, also known as grounding, is the act of being in direct contact with the earth. This means having your body or skin touching the grass, water, sand, soil, or raw conductive materials covering the ground. This means, take off your sneakers! Rubber soles prevent you from earthing. So do plastic and asphalt, and treated woods. The earth is rich in electrons, so it has a negative charge. Free radicals have a positive charge. Your body is infiltrated by free radicals from the electromagnetic radiation coming from your cell phone, microwaves, computers, WiFi, and Bluetooth devices. They are by-products that are toxic to our body and that build up. However, when earthing, they are neutralized by the negatively charged ions created by the earth. The earth grounds our bodies, just like it does the electrical outlets in our homes, where it lessens any extra positive charges. Earthing improves circulation, reduces inflammation, improves sleep, and balances your cortisol rhythm. So, next time you're out in your garden, kick off your shoes and reap the benefits of a few negative ionic energies.

In a world where expectations are diminishing and hopelessness is rising, gardening brings forth expectation and promise. Growing your herbs is an act of faith. Taking a tiny plant of the tiniest seeds and planting those seeds in the healthiest soil, tending and caring for them while they grow, and experiencing the awe in the changes that occur gives us great pause while we stand rapt in the poetic symbolism of transformation. It's like watching a child grow up and become themselves. On whichever side of the solstice we are sitting, and whichever holidays converge from the many different cultures and religions, themes of brotherhood and peace rise in the air, and you and I can think of the joy our magical gardens give us.

Our sacred places where we grow our herbs are where expectations, faith, and hope are planted. If we work hard and nurture and learn the techniques, it symbolizes our love and care, not just for our plants but also for our family, friends and neighbors. It's a reminder of our heritage, grandparents, and how much we love our family and want to provide organic, fresh, sustainable goods. It reflects our personality and character. When the daylight hours start to grow longer, we can joyfully anticipate the greenery ahead of us. Sometimes on a clear night, I go out and stand in my garden covered in snow, under the millions of stars, barefoot, and think about the herbs of happiness to come. I practice my garden rituals of thanking the Elements and express my gratitude for what is to come.

Outdoor Gardens

Whether you plan on a cottage garden, small garden, courtyard garden, or a long and narrow garden, you should plan what times of the day and where each part of the garden gets light and sun. Consider what your plans are for your garden and how you will access each part. Will you be growing vegetables with your herbs; will you have a spot nearby to enjoy a cup of coffee? Take a seat by a window or on the porch or patio and ponder the size of your lawn. Then think about the size of your garden.

It doesn't have to be square or rectangular. It can be a circle, oblong, or oval shape. Herbal plants hold their own in a formal garden design or live happily in areas where plants already exist. While you are planning the size of your garden, think about how you plan to use them. For cooking, rituals, spells, teas, etc.

You might intend to make herbal blends for gift-giving or bath favors, or maybe you have always wanted to make your own herb wreath. Whatever your dreams are, you will need to design a garden that will accommodate multiple plants. Herbal plants yield surprisingly large amounts. For regular culinary use, you may only need one tarragon, rosemary, or oregano plant. But if you plan to dry your herbs, or make a year's worth of parsley pesto, you will need more like a dozen plants. One way to narrow the playing field is to think about your spells and your cooking. If you make lots of salads, pasta, or pizza, consider multiple oregano, basil, sage, and thyme. Then again, if you love tacos, grow mint, cilantro, oregano, and marjoram. If you are a tea lover, grow some lemon balm, chamomile, mint, and pineapple sage! The ideas are endless.

Start with the Soil

Most herbs need well-drained soil. Do your research for this. You can amend the soil you already have by making a raised garden bed design. This way, you can customize the type of soil you use to suit the herbs you plan on growing. Know this: different herbs require different types of soil. For instance, rosemary, lavender, and thyme do well in alkaline soils that sharply drain. Mints and basil prefer loads of moisture and richer dirt, so you can plant them near your hose if you want.

When you start thinking about how you will arrange the herbs in your garden design, there are some basic garden fundamentals: shorter plants should be planted along the edges of the garden with the taller plants in the back. Rosemary, tarragon, dill, and fennel are examples of taller herbs, where lavenders, chives, and mints are in the mid-range category for height, and parsley, oregano, and thyme are a bit shorter. If you are grouping herbs together, remember to pair them with herbs with the same soil, sun, and water needs. So, plant your dill, lavender, rosemary, cilantro, and oregano where the most direct sunlight falls, whereas mints, sage, and parsley can handle partly shady areas. There are no other groups of plants that offer such diversity in usage as herbs. Whether for healing, spellwork, cooking, or landscaping, herbs have been grown and harvested all over the world for as long as humankind or animals have walked the earth. For me, it has taught me how to be more patient and to never give up. It's incredible how one can have total faith that something you have planted or cared for will bring such joy.

Gardening Tools

Every gardener needs to be all about hands-on work, but equipment and tools exist to help garden more efficiently, reduce calluses on our hands, and create holes in the ground for our herbs to grow much easier than digging by hand.

Important Gardening Tools Include:

1. Hand trowel
2. Garden hand fork
3. Shovel
4. Spade
5. Watering can
6. Rake
7. Garden hose
8. Garden knife
9. Wheelbarrow
10. Weeder
11. Pruning saw
12. Pruning shears
13. Mattock
14. Moisture meter
15. Hedgers
16. Hand sprayer
17. Lawn mower

USING HERBS IN YOUR MAGIC

Herbs are one of the most magical tools to use in your witchcrafting! Power is the foundation of herb magic. Power is generated and cared for by the universe, from single seed germination to the energy that rotates our planet, the energy of all living things, of birth, life, death, and rebirth. Like each crystal, each herb has its own unique vibrational energy, which, again like crystals, is determined by its chemical density and composition. These herbal powers and properties are dictated by their habitat, color, scent, design, and other aspects. The magic of herbs, therefore, is to cause needed or desired change. For maximum herbal powers, you should choose the herbs with the vibration corresponding to your specific ritual or spell. For instance, cedar will help with fertility spells but also powerfully enhances money-drawing spells.

Contrary to what many believe, a full moon is not necessary for herb rituals or spells. They can be used for magic 365 days a year during any type of weather, at any time of day or night! The only real necessities for herb magic are the seeds, herbs, flowers, and a few previously mentioned tools for gardening and grinding, including a mortar and pestle, a large bowl (wooden not metal), candles, jars, charcoal, and an incense burner, a large glass or ceramic bowl for infusions, and, of course, your sacred altar or spell table. Your herb spells are cast, and your herbs enchanted at your altar. If you are spell-casting or performing rituals outside, use a tree stump or flat rock.

Preparing yourself before engaging in herb magic is very important. Get yourself clean and relaxed in loose clothing. I always take an herbal ritual bath or add an herbal sachet to my bathwater. Then I begin creating my vision. Visualization is the essence of spell magic. I picture my intent of what I need in my mind's eye. I suggest you do the same. For magical purposes, visualization is used to form a clear picture of your intent and then direct your powers towards it, as if it has already manifested. For example, visualize that you are dating the person you are attracted to. Never forget to get the permission of others onto whom you cast spells unless the spells are in the form of gifts.

How to Create Magic with Herbs

Enchanting your herbs aligns your magical intention with the plant's vibrations. Sometimes, this calls for a single herb or a blend of them, each enchanted one by one.

1. The best way to start is by collecting herbs from the wild or those you have harvested from your garden. Speak aloud, "I am gathering these herbs for..." then place all of your gathered herbs surrounding your mixing bowl on your altar, light the appropriate corresponding colored candles, and begin the visualization process.

2. Add your herbs to your mixing bowl and run your fingers several times through the herbs while softly and slowly chanting your intention, such as "petals of rose, petals of rose, bring to my life a love that grows."

3. Now enchanted, your herbs are ready for spellwork, or to be placed in spell jars to put around your home, etc. You can infuse edible herbs in boiling water, but it has to be in Pyrex, not metal. Keep the water covered so that no steam escapes. Let steep one teaspoon of herbs for every one cup of water, and then strain before using. You can also use a cheesecloth for bathing, making teas, and anointing your body.

Incense

Incense is a combination of any herb materials, which are then mixed together with charcoal. Burning aromatic resins and herbs is traditional around the world and has been for thousands of years. They not only smell good, but they are also used for healing ceremonies, purification, and for cleansing sacred areas. For magical purposes, incense is used in spellwork for its vibrations along with visualization, and can also be used for rituals and background vibrations during healing treatments. Ground your herbs in your mortar and pestle, light a charcoal block in your abalone shell, cauldron, or incense burner, and sprinkle small amounts of your herb incense onto the charcoal every couple of minutes while casting your spell.

Herbal Garden Incense Recipe from My Own Garden

This recipe, inspired by herbs I grew and harvested from my garden, is a blend of lemongrass, rosemary, and lavender.

What You'll Need:

- 1¾ teaspoon ground Salvia rosmarinus (rosemary)
- 1 tablespoon ground Cymbopogon citratus (lemongrass)
- 2 teaspoons ground Lavandula angustifolia (lavender)
- 1¼ tablespoon water

Steps

1. Grind the herbs into a powder.
2. Mix the powders.
3. Add 6 drops of water slowly, and each time mash the mixture with the back of a spoon, pressing them together, not stirring.
4. Eventually, a dough will form. You want it to be fairly dry, just moist enough to hold it together.
5. Once the dough is formed and holds together, pinch

off a small amount and form it into a cone shape.
(Make it skinny and tall).

6. Let your cones dry for at least one week on a flat
surface. They have to be entirely dried out before they
will burn. Light the tip of the cone with a flame and let
it burn until it is smoking.

7. Place your cone on your incense burner!

Casting a Circle

Many modern-day witchcraft spells call for casting a circle. In
its basic form, a circle is a sacred space visualized by the practitioner, their ritual tools, and their altar during spellcrafting.
Most magicians think of the sacred circle as an energy container
from within which they practice their craft. It is a spiritual
protection shield from all things negative during the open
emotional and vulnerable state necessary for spellwork. It is like
an impenetrable invisible force field from which imbalance,
disharmony, and negativity bounce off. Before you cast your
circle, take a moment to clear all negative energy and then
follow these steps:

How to Cast a Circle

1. Use one of your homemade incense to smoke the area
where you will cast your circle.

2. Think carefully about your space and location. It can
be as large or small as you desire. You can mentally and
visually map out your circle with candles and crystals

to mark the directions (N-S-E-W) and the corresponding Elements or directions.

3. Mark a pentacle if you include the Spirit Element in your pattern, otherwise using a cross pattern North (Earth), Air (East), Fire (South), and Water (West).

4. Start casting your circle by facing East and calling upon the Air Element. Moving clockwise, you will end up with the Earth element facing North.

5. North is where your ritual begins.

6. Start relaxing by using deep breathing techniques, center yourself, be calm and present.

7. Start visualizing the earth under your feet, earthing you, and chant, "I call upon you, Earth Element."

8. Moving clockwise (eastward), picture the wind swirling about you, "Element of Air, I call upon you."

9. Moving clockwise (southward), picture flames surrounding you and call upon the warming presence of the sun, "Element of Fire, I call upon you."

10. Turning westward, visualize waves, waterfalls, rivers, and streams, "Element of Water, I call upon you."

11. Moving back to the North spot of your circle, visualize your feet sending pillars of light deep down, all the way to the earth's core.

12. Pull the earth's energy from its core into your soul and throughout your body, creating a light flowing about you in a circle - "Under the spirit of the Earth, Wind, Water, and Fire, I cast this circle of protection below, above, and within."

13. Now your circle is sacred and ready for ritual.

Circle Tips

If you step out of your circle before you have finished your ritual, create a cut motion with your wand or blade across the circle's boundary and chant, "I open a door using my wand." The energy from your wand will direct you toward the open path. When you re-enter, use the same process to close the door.

Closing/Opening Your Circle

Closing or opening a sacred circle is a technique for showing gratitude to the Elements for helping you cast your intentions. Start the closing ritual by facing North and chant, "Farewell, Earth; I thank thee for thy energy." Next, release the water, facing westward, "Farewell, Water, I thank thee for thy energy." Turning southward, "Farewell, Fire, I thank thee for thy energy." Facing East, "Farewell, Air, I thank thee for thy energy." End back at the North point, "I bid you farewell, oh spirits of the world. I close this circle and send the energy back into the ground.

Jar and Bottle Magic

Without a doubt, there are zillions of ways to work and make magic. Magic practice takes many forms, running from a simple spoken charm to elaborately formulated rituals. This has been the way throughout the history of magic and across the various witchcraft traditions we have been taught. One historical and popular means of creative magic is the vessel, bottle, and jar spell. A vessel spell is a magical item created by the magician using some type of sealed bottle, jar, or other vessel, often with wax or a cork seal. These vessels are a part of many regional, folkloric, and cultural magical protocols and serve many different intentions.

Examples of bottle and jar charms are mentioned across Europe and the United States. They have been documented in grimoires, the Book of Shadows, and Black Books around the globe. Spell jars have survived in the folk customs of Hoodoo and continue to grow in popularity among magic practitioners of many modern-day spellcrafts. They are inexpensive to make with easy-to-find materials. They don't require much physical maintenance, and the spells continue to work for as long as the jar is sealed. It is a favorite practice among traditional practitioners, as the spells have remained mostly unchanged throughout the years. No longer are they just part of black and red magic. Many love spells, money spells, and others are performed as vessel rituals without any curses or hexes being involved, especially since herbs, crystals, oils, and vinegar meet the needs of so many magical goals.

Herbal Sachet Magic

While your herbal garden is good enough to eat and make potions, these wonderfully aromatic herbs can be tucked into sachets whose fragrance will carry you right back to the glory of your garden. You can use them to scent clothing in your dryer, a drawer, or even put one under your pillow. You don't have to be a seamstress either. You can purchase mesh bags, ready-made, and fill them with your dried herbs. Just tie them up and enjoy. On average, it only takes about 30-45 minutes to make your sachets. It all depends on how extravagant you want to get. Just gather your materials, and you will have gifts for the holidays and a family that smiles every time they open a drawer or retrieve their clothes from the dryer.

Follow the directions I gave you on how to dry your herbs and enjoy experimenting with them. It is essential to know when to harvest and dry out your herbs quickly to preserve their fragrance. Here are some easy steps for making your herbal sachets:

1. Blend enough of your herbs into the bag you have chosen for your sachet.
2. Place several drops of matching essential oils on your blend.
3. Fill your sachet with your blended herbs and essential oils.
4. Glue, sew or tie the sachet closed.
5. Wrap a nice string or ribbon around the sealed top of the sachet.
6. ENJOY!

Dressing Candles

When using herbs for candle dressing, start by thoroughly drying out the plant material. Otherwise, it can mildew and leave an awful scent. Finely crush your herbs in your mortar and pestle to release their aroma. You can also steep your ground herbs in heated wax for a few hours so that the herbal essence penetrates and becomes incorporated into the wax. Then strain the wax before you make your candle. Another way is to add the ground or chopped herbs as you pour your candle. This makes a beautiful design in your herbal candle projects, especially if they are colorful. At this point, you are probably thinking about the best herbs for dressing your candles. The same herbs used in aromatherapy evoke emotions and calmness and are also the most popular herbs for candles. The leaves and flowers are also used to dress the outside of your candles.

Lavender is one of the most popular candle herbs. Lavender reduces anxiety and elicits calm and relaxed feelings. Use the flowers to decorate the outside and infuse the grounded powder with your wax. Mint-scented candles, from spearmint to peppermint, make perfect gifts and centerpieces for holidays. Burn spearmint-infused candles year-round to cleanse your home of negativity and promote clarity of mind. Rosemary works well for its aroma and as a dressing design for your candles. Harvest the leaves or grow them in the same container you are going to make your candle in. Steep the leaves in a tight glass container, covered for three days. Chamomile has both decorative and aromatic values for candle-making. Lemon verbena is one of the most aromatic citrus-scented leaves there are. Place the leaves separately on screens and then store them in zippered bags. Keep all of your herbs in airtight containers.

Essential Oil Making

Coarsely chopped, dried herbs create soothing essential oil infusions. It is important to use dried herbs. The best choices for oils are olive and sunflower. The oil should be fresh so that the aromatic infusion will last the longest. Olive and sunflower oils are good choices. Be sure to use fresh oil so that the infusion will last longer.

What You'll Need:

- Canning jars or any glass jar with a lid works nicely.
- A cheesecloth, strainer, or a fine-weave towel.
- Amber glass makes your infusion last much longer because it blocks out light.

Herb-infused oil steps:

1. Make sure your jar is very dry and clean. Any water will spoil the oil.
2. Fill the jar to the top with herbs.
3. Slowly pour the oil over the herbs.
4. Move the herbs around slowly with a chopstick, making sure there are no air pockets.

5. Add enough oil to cover the herbs completely, fill the jar to the brim.

6. Cover the jar and shake it a couple of times.

7. Put your jar in a cool, dry place.

8. Every so often, shake your jar.

9. Your oil will be ready in about two months.

10. Strain the oil into your amber-colored storage bottles using a cheesecloth.

11. Squeeze the herbs over the cloth to get that last bit of herbal goodness.

12. Add one capsule of vitamin E to the oil.

13. Place a lid or cork on your bottles and label them. They will last up to two years.

PART 2:

THE SPELLS

In this section, spells will include all of the education provided in Part 1. From Love Spells to Health Spells, to Money Spells, to Protection Spells, herbs are healthy and magical to their very essence, and are beautiful. They are full of ways to practice healing and protection magic, as well as dressing candles, and do-it-yourself essential oil-making. They are the most ancient way to make your space sacred. But the most powerful way to use your herbs is by using them in your magic. Whether for love or healing, abundance or success, you can harness their natural energy for many of your mystical endeavors. Part 2 will fill your enquiring mind with spells from A to Z.

8

LOVE SPELLS

Long before movies, romance novels, and self-help books on how to attract that special someone, magical practitioners took matters into their own hands. The lovestruck, lovelorn, and the romantically loved turned to folk wisdom gathered from generations passed to keep and catch romance. Plants and herbs have been symbolizing devotion and love for centuries. The ancient Greeks wove marigolds and mint into wreaths and bridal garlands. Long ago in Italy, brides carried rosemary to be sure of the groom's fertility, and wheat for their own. During medieval times in Europe, brides carried chives and gals and other pungent herbs to ward off evil spirits that might try to disrupt their happiness. Furthermore, during the Victorian era, pansies, roses, marjoram, and lavender were combined for contentment and romantic success (aka love spells). Most love spells call for unique ingredients that have to be used in combination with specific sets of arcane words.

Love potions are documented as far as the Greeks of ancient times adding ground-up orchids to their wine for its aphrodisiac properties. They believed this potion would stimulate passionate love for whoever drank it. It was so popular among the Greeks that the sacred orchid became temporarily extinct. Versions of the Blister Beetle or Spanish Fly drink are still created today. Historically, true Spanish Fly was made from a substance called cantharidin, which is produced by blister beetles. When in contact with the skin, cantharidin caused blistering, hence the name. Spanish Fly has been traced back to an Empress in Rome, who used cantharidin for sexual purposes so she could then use the act for blackmail. It was also used for orgies by Roman gladiators. Unfortunately, what wasn't known by those unsuspecting lovers was that the warmth and swelling of the genitals was not stimulation but inflammation!

Magical textbooks in 16th century Europe also became increasingly popular. Once such book was entitled, *The Book of Secrets of Albertus Magnus: Of the Virtues of Herbs, Stones, and Certain Beasts*. One of his potions was made by mixing periwinkle with crushed earthworms, which was to stimulate affection between a married couple. Around that same time, animal products coupled with herbs also became common ingredients in love potions. Ingredients from snake fat, bat's blood, pigeon's heart, and sparrow heads were among them.

These spells don't require finding archaeological remains, and mine don't incorporate bat's blood or sparrow heads. One love spell asked the user to have a brass ring inscribed with the name of the Goddess of Love seated on a rooftop with a lotus in their hands chanting magical words at the moon. These spells do, however, require the tender loving care of your plants. Even if there is a blooming romance, love spells with all of their herbaceousness can influence the chemistry between you and your romantic partner in ways that create long-lasting fidelity, loyalty, and lust. I have made the following love spells to meet your specific circumstances, so take great care before you use them and consider your intentions carefully.

Bringing Love into Your Life Spell

Magical herbs are commonly used for creating love ties, often practiced by green witches. Sometimes, love ties are cast by blowing powdered herbs onto a candle's flame while performing ritual chants. Magnolia, Thyme, Rose, Rosemary, Verbena, Vanilla, and Violet are some of the herbs usually taking part in spells to bring love into your life.

HOW LONG IT TAKES:

1 hour

WHAT YOU'LL NEED:

- A basil plant you planted yourself in your living room
- Large pot
- Soil
- Dried basil leaves
- Dried leaves of lavender
- Red rose petals
- ½ teaspoon honey
- One red candle and lighter
- Rose essential oil
- A saucepan
- A small wooden stick or spoon
- A piece of paper
- A red ink pen or fine marker
- One piece of thin red ribbon
- A small clay bowl with a lid

- A thin red ribbon

STEPS:

1. Put your basil plant in the same room where you will be casting the spell.
2. On a large altar or spell table, light your red candle and ask the Sun Goddess or call upon the Element of Fire for its powers to bring love into your life.
3. Write your loved one's full name on the piece of paper, leaving room above it for your name. This way, the two of you will be joined with one on top of the other.
4. On the front of the paper, rewrite the two names all the way to the bottom.
5. On the back of the paper, neatly write: "I call upon the Element of Fire and the powers of animal magnetism to bind your heart as well as your feelings. Only me will you think of, and for only me will you feel love. The essence of each herb powered by the light of fire will be the fuel to our relationship as it will grow like the plant, always leafy and full of love. As it is and should be."
6. While the burning candle is doing its magic by the Element of Fire, start chopping the leaves of each herb, one at a time, and placing them in the saucepan.
7. Focus on the face of your love interest the entire time you are chopping herbs. Picture your future as if you are already living it. Picture making wonderful

memories as you project your intention into the saucepan.

8. After all of the leaves of your herbs are chopped and in the saucepan, toss in your honey, hence keeping your love interest always sweet to you.

9. Place in your rose oil and mix with your wooden spoon.

10. Fold your spell written on the piece of paper and place it in the bottom of the clay pot.

11. Pour the mixture over the spell and cover the clay pot.

12. Tie the piece of red ribbon around the clay pot.

13. Bury your pot deep in the ground somewhere in your yard.

14. Once the spell has taken hold, and you are now with your loved one, or your present relationship has blossomed, dig up the clay pot and replace it with the basil plant you have been caring for from the start.

15. As your basil plant thrives, so will your relationship.

16. Thank the elements and the plant.

It's All About Loving Yourself Spell

It has to be about loving yourself first before the magic can be made at all. We live in a world of emotional struggles, comparisons, self-image, and societal pressures. If you have lost love and respect for yourself because of some emotional trauma, a failure, or a bad heartbreak, this is the time for some self-love magic. Self-love spells can be the happiest and best magic there is for living a positive life. Too often, the focus is on loving others or wanting others to love us. Without self-love, it's impossible to show another person any real, true, or profound emotions. One of the most powerful ways to do this comes from nature, so this is one of my special herbs spells for self-love magic.

HOW LONG IT TAKES:

35 minutes

WHAT YOU'LL NEED:

- A mirror
- 3 pink candles
- 3 blue candles
- Lavender
- Rose petals
- Chamomile
- Mint

STEPS:

1. Place your mirror on your altar.
2. Place your candles around the mirror in a circle.
3. Put all of the herbs in your cupped hands and begin rubbing them between your fingers while feeling their energy.
4. Close your eyes and visualize yourself where you are sitting.
5. Imagine and picture in your mind a green ball of energy glowing in the middle of your chest.
6. Visualize the green light ball growing brighter and livelier and beginning to mix with the candle lights that are reflecting in the mirror and then against you.
7. Take several slow and deep breaths, exhaling.
8. While deep breathing, scatter the herbs onto the mirror and chant:

> *Love within, without a doubt*
> *All of my pain on its way out*
> *Heal my scars so that I may breathe*
> *No longer will I feel any thoughts that*
>   *seethe*
> *As it is and should be*

Dreaming of Me Spell

The best way to use a spell about dreaming is to have the person wanting you with their free will. Magically getting a love interest or loved one to dream about you is not an easy feat. You have to free your mind of your own problems before you can influence another person's dreams. It also helps to put the thought of you into their mind before they go to sleep. Prior to your spellwork, some techniques are to call or text them before they go to sleep. Leave a picture of yourself near them at bedtime, burn incense familiar to you, or any other mystical ideas you can come up with to stir the unconscious of the person upon whom you are casting your spell.

HOW LONG IT TAKES:

40 minutes

WHAT YOU'LL NEED:

- Rosemary
- Lavender
- Cotton material
- Cotton
- Parchment paper
- Needle and thread

STEPS:

1. Cut two pieces of cotton fabric and sew them closed on three sides (you are making a dream pillow).
2. Stuff your pillow with cotton.
3. Add your herbs.
4. Sew the pillow closed.
5. Write the person's name and precisely what you want them to dream about on the parchment paper.
6. Prepare your altar with crystals and rosemary.
7. Cast a sacred circle (see casting a circle in the previous chapter) big enough for you and your altar to be in the middle.
8. Stand in the middle and place the parchment paper on top of the pillow.
9. Hold the pillow in your hands and chant:

> **Blessed Earth, may this be**
> **Send (person's name) dreams of me**
> **Awaken their mind, as I hold the key**
> **My voice, my heart, my soul, they can see**
> **As it is and should be**

10. Place the pillow in the bedroom dresser drawer of the person upon whom you are casting the dream spell, where it can't be detected.

How Sweet Love is Spell (to Sweeten your Relationship)

The theory behind this honey jar spell is relatively simple. You use honey and a handwritten note that encourages both of you in a relationship to be more loving, kinder, and sweeter towards each other. The wonderful thing about jar magic is that it is very portable, meaning you can take your spell with you wherever you go if you are inclined to do so. Honey jar magic is a lovely example of sympathetic and gentle magic. It can also be used to sweeten any relationship, such as to make your boss sweeter, create a more loving relationship with family members, or even for a problematic neighbor.

HOW LONG IT TAKES:

1 hour

WHAT YOU'LL NEED:

I like to use a clear glass honey jar, but you can use pink too. Make sure the mouth of the jar is large enough for your ingredients. Pick a jar that you have meditated on while thinking about the person upon whom you are casting your spell. Make sure the lip can handle the heat of a candle.

- Honey or molasses
- Paper
- A pen
- Cardamom

- Lavender
- Rose
- Cinnamon
- Small red candle

STEPS:

1. Write the name of the person with whom you want to sweeten your relationship THREE times on your paper.

2. Rotate the paper 90 degrees.

3. Over the top of the person's name in a cross-type manner, since you rotated the paper, write your name THREE times. Your name will cross the other name like a grid.

4. Close your eyes and take 6 breaths in through your nose and out of your mouth, slowly.

5. With your eyes slowly opening, focus on the paper with the names. Think specifically about how you want the relationship to be sweeter (romantically, sexually, friendly, compassionate, etc.).

6. Focus strongly on your intention.

7. Using your pen, write your intention in a circle around the grid of names, making sure to connect the circle so it is sealed with the words (last word written to the first word written). I am not the best at writing in cursive, so don't worry if it looks messy, even if you write love in a circle over and over again.

8. You can add symbols or sigils; embellish your paper as you wish.

9. Fold the paper in half in the same direction as you wrote the other person's name.

10. Turn the paper 90 degrees and fold it in half again in the direction your name is written.

11. Anoint your parcel with drops of lavender oil.

12. Place your parcel in the jar and fill it with honey.

13. Add your herbs.

14. Stick your finger through the herbs and honey until you are touching your parcel and chant:

> *Sacred honey from the bee,*
> *Your sweetened powers, please lend to me*
> *Just as this honey is sweet*
> *So sweet shall (person's name) be with me*
> *As it is and should be*

15. Touch your finger, covered in honey, to your lips.

16. Visualize the person's face as you lick the honey from your lips.

17. Close the jar with the heat-resistant lid.

18. Place your red candle on top of your jar.

19. Think about your spell with deep intention and light the candle.

20. Let the candle burn down all the way.

21. Leave the candle wax on the jar and store it in a safe place.

22. Go back to your jar frequently to look at it and thank it for its power.

I prefer to charge my spell jar twice a month, each time with a new candle. I rotate between red and white, restating my intention, so my spell stays strong. As you can tell, I am an herb-loving magical practitioner, and every time I write a spell for you or me, I learn something new.

Think of Me Spell

This is a simple but very effective spell and will help you keep your loved one connected with you! This magic ritual is effective and mighty, and once cast, there is no turning back, so be very clear about your intentions. Archangel Chamuel is the angle of nurturance in romantic love. He is often called upon for spells regarding relationships, restoring love, and understanding unconditional love. Ask yourself how strong you want your spell to be. Do you want someone obsessed and thinking non-stop about you? Do you want someone to start thinking about you more and more as each day passes? Do you have a crush and want thoughts of you to pop into your love interest's head? These are the questions you need to ask yourself before casting this spell.

HOW LONG IT TAKES:

15 minutes

WHAT YOU'LL NEED:

- A piece of white paper
- A red pen
- Basil
- Mint
- Lemon balm

STEPS:

1. Write the name of the person you are casting the spell on with a red pen.

2. Chop up your herbs.

3. Place them in the center of the paper.

4. Fold it into a parcel so that the herbs do not fall out.

5. Hold the parcel in your right hand and repeat the person's name three times.

6. Chant:

> *Help me, most powerful Archangel Chamuel to have (name of person) think of (your name) often. Through his powerful magic that only (your name) is the object of (person's name) thoughts of affection. To call me while lying down tonight and ask me to spend a life together. As it is and should be.*

7. Put the folded parcel under your pillow and repeat the person's name three times.

8. Do this for three nights and then hide it somewhere where it will not be disturbed.

Repair This Relationship Spell

Relationships are hopeful and made up of wonderful connections between a couple, family members, or friends. They are meant to be your personal love and protection support team. Whether meeting someone you are in a relationship with happened by chance or it was predetermined before this life cycle started, the timeline in every relationship always stands a chance of having separation, arguments, disagreements, or a rift between those involved. Sometimes, these rifts are learning lessons that help us grow and move forward in life, giving us lessons to take into the future. While these rifts can hurt at times, they don't have to be permanent. I created this spell to reconnect loved ones, friends, and family members who have let a rift make them forget what it feels like to have a sacred love connection.

HOW LONG IT TAKES:

30 minutes

WHAT YOU'LL NEED:

- Sage bundle for smudging
- Hawthorn dried and powdered (Crataegus spp.)
- Rose petals dried and powdered (Rosa rugosa)
- Motherwort dried and powdered (Leonurus cardiaca) or Lemon balm (Melissa officinalis)
- 1 white taper candle
- 1 pink candle

- Wooden toothpick
- Parchment paper
- Lighter

STEPS:

1. Clean your items and your sacred space by smudging them with sage.
2. Grind up your herbs into a powder.
3. Keeping the wick intact, break the white candle in half (if it is for two people, otherwise break it into sections according to how many people are involved in the rift.
4. With your wooden toothpick, scribe the name of each person into separate sections of the broken candle. While scribing, visualize the Earth grounding any negative energies of that person so they can return to their pure state.
5. Lay the broken white candle on the parchment paper and chant:

> *We have seen the bad weather*
> *Now it's time to come back together*

6. Light the pink candle.
7. Sprinkle one herb at a time into the candle flame and notice the beautiful sparks.

8. Drip the wax from the pink candle into the cracks of the white candle.

9. As the pink wax is repairing the cracks, picture in your mind's eye loving pink energy, and those involved being connected by the wick, as the pink wax is strengthening the connection once again.

10. When the cracks are repaired, let the wax harden.

11. Visualize the white candle with a glowing and loving pink light surrounding it.

12. Visualize the person(s) you had the rift with surrounded by the same pink light.

13. Chant:

> *All is mended*
> *All is well*
> *Reunited we are*
> *My words do tell*
> *As it is and should be*

14. When you feel the spell is complete, light the candle and let it burn all the way down.

Relationship Passion Restoration Spell

Sometimes the spark in your relationship starts to dwindle or even feels lost. Rejuvenating the passion and restoring the romantic spark in your relationship is exactly what this spell was created to do. If things between you and your partner have been tough, you are not alone. One of the most challenging times that most long-term relationships face is a decline of passion and initial attraction. You can smooth this rough patch and get things back to hugs and kisses with my Passion Restoring Relationship spell.

HOW LONG IT TAKES:

Full moon overnight + 30 minutes

WHAT YOU'LL NEED:

- Full moon
- Cinnamon
- Vanilla
- 2 red candles
- 2 pink candles
- 2 white candles
- Red cellophane
- 1 elastic band
- 1 glass of water
- Lavender essence
- 1 red rose

STEPS:

1. Put your water in the center of your altar.
2. Place the red rose in the water.
3. Add your herbs.
4. Place the water with the rose and herbs under a full moon.
5. Put your bowl of water, rose petals, and herbs on your altar.
6. Light your candles in a circle around the bowl.
7. Focus on your candles and place three drops of lavender essence in the water while thinking of passionate love-making with your partner, and becoming one.
8. Do this for three minutes and then chant three times:

> *I call upon the passion of the moon*
> *Ignite the love between us two*
> *Together in love none too soon*
> *For romance, hugs, and kisses true*
> *As it is and should be*

Hands Off Spell (for removing unwanted affection)

The usage of garlic magnifies this Hands Off Spell tenfold! Sometimes it just happens. You want to be friends, but the other person wants more. They start clinging and constantly touching, even when they know it makes you uncomfortable. It is quite selfish, if you think about it. I remember when I was in school, I had a really nice friend. We would do our homework together, and talk about sports and psychology. Then he said to me that he wanted more from our friendship. I felt heartbroken. Darn, I knew I was going to lose my good friend. I told him I never wanted to take a chance on ruining our friendship. He said he accepted that but began moving closer and closer every chance he got. I could even smell his breath. I had to turn to my Black Book in the hopes of magic that would maintain our friendship without me ever having to smell his breath again or be uncomfortable from having him lean against my body every time he was about to leave.

HOW LONG IT TAKES:

10 minutes

WHAT YOU'LL NEED:

- Garlic oil
- Pen
- Paper
- Black candle
- Abalone shell

STEPS:

1. Write the name of the person producing the unwanted affection on a piece of white paper with a black pen.
2. Light your black candle.
3. Place three drops of garlic oil on the name written on the paper.
4. While smelling the garlic, think of how annoying this person's advances have become. Feel the aggravation and repulsion.
5. Hold the paper over the flame (being careful) until it lights on fire.
6. Drop it into your abalone shell.
7. Chant 10 times:

> *Friends we'll be*
> *Without you touching me*
> *So mote it be*

8. Let it burn until it goes out.
9. Drip the black wax over the ashes.
10. Dig a small hole in the dirt in your yard and dump the waxed ashes and cover it up.

~

Confidence of a Lion Spell

There are many reasons for a person to lack confidence. A bad experience, the way we were raised, being bullied. It is never your fault for why you are experiencing low self-confidence. The good news is that it is not a permanent state of being. This spell should be coupled with increased exercise (releases endorphins) and possibly a mani-pedi, which goes for both sexes.

HOW LONG IT TAKES:

35 minutes

WHAT YOU'LL NEED:

- Fennel seed
- Dogwood
- Curry
- Olive oil
- Small glass bowl
- Yellow candle
- Blue candle
- Mirror
- Pen and paper

STEPS:

1. Place your glass bowl in the center of your altar.
2. Rub the herbs in your hands until warm while smelling their aroma.

3. Place the herbs in the bowl and cover with olive oil (I like to use good regular olive oil for this spell, not virgin).

4. Put a candle on each side of the bowl.

5. Anoint your candles by touching the herbal olive oil and rubbing it on the sides of the candles.

6. Light both candles.

7. Write down five positive affirmations on the paper every ten minutes while the candles burn.

8. The spell is most powerful if you complete step 7 six times while looking in the mirror.

9. After reading the affirmations six times (after every ten minutes), snuff out your candles or let them burn down.

10. Lift the bowl gently, put the affirmations underneath the bowl, and let the herbs and oil magnify the words.

11. Leave it there until your confidence soars. You can make a small altar anywhere if you need to use your main altar and the bowl is in the way.

HEALTH SPELLS

The synchronicity between religion, magic, and medical practice becomes rather noticeable when one looks into ancient text and old scripts. Before the foundation of medical schools, monasteries and convents were the epicenters of medical practice and knowledge for thousands of years. Alongside the scientific development of medicine, which is rooted in the oldest of sciences, is the practice of folk medicine, most of all the herbal medicines, which are the original foundation and form of modern-day pharmacology. Recently, the number of people using herbal health practices, either in combination with others or alone, has risen dramatically. An herbal "renaissance" is occurring globally. The World Health Organization (WHO) reported that ¾ of the world's population use herbs for their basic health and wellness on a daily basis [1]. Furthermore, many pharmaceutical/conventional medicines distributed worldwide are made directly from both traditional remedies and nature. More than 50,000 species are used for herbal remedies, and some of these are facing extinction because of overexploitation.

Medicines such as morphine, quinine, and codeine all contain ingredients that are plant derivatives. These drugs, albeit synthetically manufactured, have become important to the lives of many of those who are sick and suffering. Isn't it wonderful to have nature on our side? Did you know that the ginkgo tree is appraised as a living fossil, with fossils found that are as old as 270 million years? The ginkgo tree can live to be 3000 years old. There is, however, a note of caution. Many herbs carry the same potential side effects and risks as manufactured drugs, and most are sold with unresearched promises. The good news here is that most teas and herbs offer many ways of improving our health, so do your homework about the effectiveness, safety issues, and potential interactions, especially for pregnant and breastfeeding mothers, as well as infants and children.

Herbs' magical and spiritual power has been documented for thousands of years through observation and use. These herbal allies' purposes and magical properties have been cherished more and more as people have learned about their growing conditions and natural habitats, how they are used for healing, and by analyzing their colors, scents, and flavors. Throughout millennia and experience, magicians and others have attributed specific qualities and energies to specific herbs. Both modern and ancient cultures have used herbs to repel negative energy and attract the positive. Magical crafters hang charms and poppets, make amulets, create perfumes and incense, blend potions and elixirs, and provide offerings to deities. From incense to smudging, witches have learned how to harness the power of herbs for health and wellness, protection and wisdom, and any imaginable purpose.

Bad Vibes Begone Spell (for releasing negative energy)

Each of us draws energy from a variety of sources to nourish our emotional needs. This is also how we power up the cells in our bodies, raise our cortisol levels, and metabolize cells, depending on emotional triggers. There are herbs specific to this process that have been used for centuries, and their frequencies directly impact transforming and deflecting negative energies. The worrisome thing about negativity is that you can only feel it; you can't see it. The good news is that you can eliminate it! Negativity can bring disharmony, lower your self-confidence, create emotional turmoil, and ruin peacefulness.

HOW LONG IT TAKES:

15 minutes

WHAT YOU'LL NEED:

- Basil
- Black pepper
- Cayenne
- Black tourmaline crystal
- Smoky quartz crystal
- Black onyx crystal
- White candle

STEPS:

1. Keeping a basil plant or plants will help you form stronger connections with the spirit world.

2. Place the crystals near your front door entrance on a shelf or small table.

3. Sprinkle black pepper on your doorstep at dusk to keep out unwanted intruders.

4. Light a white candle on your altar and sprinkle cayenne into the flame.

5. Clap three times.

6. Snuff out the candle.

～

Bad Habit No More Spell

Are you trying to rid yourself of a bad habit, like smoking or your carb intake? At some point in our lives, all of us conclude that certain behaviors, when repetitive, no longer serve us and become unhealthy. They usually begin as innocent activities, but then with time, they take over places in our lives where they were never intended to be. The longer we take to break the cycle, the more the bad habit becomes entrenched within us. By the time you realize how destructive this habit has become in your life, ridding yourself of it can seem insurmountable. Let me help you dig your way out of this problem with my Bad Habit No More Spell.

HOW LONG IT TAKES:

2 weeks

WHAT YOU'LL NEED:

- Full moon
- One box
- Paper and pen
- 2 rosemary sprigs
- 1 garlic clove
- One handful of graveyard dirt
- 1 roll of pennies
- 4-6 nails and a hammer
- 1 example or symbol of your bad habit (could be a

cigarette, a twinkie, wine bottle cork, or a cuss word
written down)

- Shovel

STEPS:

1. This spell requires commitment, as quitting any
   pattern in life does. It is very powerful but can also be
   quite tedious.
2. Meditate on your certainty about quitting your bad
   habit. It requires that you are positive and you wish to
   quit.
3. On the paper, write a list of reasons for wanting to
   stop. Keep it close by for reflection.
4. Decorate your box with a skull and bones and project
   your intent into it.
5. Leave your box outside under a full moon overnight to
   charge it.
6. Place it on your altar the following day.
7. You do not have to quit immediately. However, each
   time your bad habit tempts you, drop a penny in the
   box. If you are not at home, drop your penny or
   pennies in your box as soon as you arrive home.
8. Do this for two weeks. In the first few days, you will
   probably be dropping a lot of pennies in the box, but
   by the end of the two weeks, the number of pennies
   will significantly decrease.

9. Following the full moon, on night one of the waning moon, add your garlic clove and rosemary to your box.

10. Hold your bad habit symbol cupped in both hands. It may be matches, a candy wrapper, a dollhouse rocking chair, or a potato (to banish laziness). Get creative.

11. Take five minutes to grieve over your symbol. After all, it is like getting rid of a good friend.

12. Place your symbol in your box and seal your box with nails.

13. Take your box, shovel, nails, hammer, and graveyard dirt away from your home.

14. Dig a hole and put your box in the hole.

15. Throw your graveyard dirt on top.

16. Walk away without ever looking back.

17. Consider this as having had a funeral for your bad habit.

Restore Energy with a Peaceful Sleep Spell

Sometimes, even with enough sleep, we still feel like the energy is zapped from our bodies. Once in a while, I can get a good six to seven hours of sleep at night, and I exercise at the gym twice a week and do yoga at least three times a week, but somehow I still feel lethargic during the day. I wondered what was zapping my energy and what I should do about it. This spell worked wonders for me, but even better when I combined it with my Now I Lay Me Down To Sleep Spell, which is in my last book, *The Crystal Magic Spell Book*. I will put another spell I crafted to pair with this spell here because the two go hand in hand with the added power of peaceful dreams for energy magic.

HOW LONG IT TAKES:

20 minutes

WHAT YOU'LL NEED:

- Same rose quartz
- Chamomile tea
- 3 dried lavender stems

STEPS:

1. Sit in your bed in a comfortable position.
2. Prepare your chamomile tea.
3. With your eyes closed, gently move the rose quartz crystal around in your hands until you feel it warming.

Let its energy pass through your hands and throughout your whole body.

4. Stir your tea with the lavender stems 9 times in a sunwise (clockwise) direction.

5. Start sipping your tea.

6. Send this warming and sedating energy down to your stomach, all the way to your toes.

7. Allow your mind to settle into a peaceful state.

8. After a moment, quietly chant:

> *Calming peace come to me*
> *For tomorrow, it is the energy I need*
> *Grant restful sleep tonight*
> *Tomorrow I will be full of fight*
> *As it is and should be*

Give Me Energy, Give Me Strength Spell

This spell is for the day after the Restore My Energy with a Peaceful Sleep Spell.

HOW LONGIT TAKES:

15 - 30 minutes

WHAT YOU'LL NEED:

- Rose quartz crystal
- Dried vervain (Verbena officinalis)
- Your favorite music or song

STEPS:

1. Light the vervain.
2. Place your crystal next to it.
3. Turn up the music.
4. Start moving around and lose yourself in the music for as long as you feel, but not less than 6 minutes.

Creatively Creative Spell

Artfulness comes in many forms. Creating something wonderful that started as a tiny spec of an idea is truly magical. Creative thinking is manifestation at its deepest level. I'm not just referring to making a scrapbook or sculpting a clay pot - all creativity is a magical manifestation. Being creative can be a bit tricky, as it seems to come and go. Sometimes our creativity seems to come out of left field when we didn't know we had a creative purpose at that very moment, like when I am sitting at a stoplight. I love this spell, but it does take time, care, and nurturing. With each passing day, your creativity will grow.

HOW LONG IT TAKES:

1 month

WHAT YOU'LL NEED:

- Small piece of paper
- Seed of your choice
- Garden pot

STEPS:

1. Write your intended result for your creative project or plan on a piece of paper. Write these words when you feel filled with excitement over your plan. Use first-person and present tense, as if it has already manifested.

2. Prepare your garden pot with rich soil.

3. Dig a hole in the center of the soil.

4. Fold up your paper and stick it in the hole.

5. Place your seed next to the paper in the hole.

6. Cover your intention and the seed with rich potting soil.

7. Every time you water the plant, speak aloud your intention.

8. The manifestation will grow stronger as the plant begins to grow, until your desired result is achieved.

9. If your results are not what you expected, trust that it is for your highest good, and only good will come out of this spell.

Away with Illness Potion Spell

We are a culture that thrives on every technique, strategy, method, and motivation to ward off illness. Preventative medicine, a modern term, has been around since the beginning of time. "An apple a day keeps the doctor away." We take our vitamins every day, exercise, and stay hydrated. Some of our loved ones are too young or too old to keep up with a daily regimen of health and wellness activities, so a bit of magic goes a long way. I keep a constant supply of this magical potion, and it has worked wonders for my family and me for decades, especially during the cold and flu seasons.

HOW LONG IT TAKES:

20 minutes

WHAT YOU'LL NEED:

- 2 tablespoons grated ginger
- 2 tablespoons thyme
- Pinch of cayenne
- 2 tablespoons rosemary
- 1 teaspoon turmeric
- 2 tablespoons oregano
- Juice of 1 lemon
- 13 drops dragon's oil
- 1 teaspoon honey
- Water

STEPS:

1. Add ginger, turmeric, cayenne, rosemary, thyme, and oregano to a small saucepan.
2. Cover with water.
3. Boil for 10 minutes until the water is darkened.
4. Strain the potion.
5. Add the juice of one lemon.
6. Add honey.
7. Add 25 drops of dragon's blood.
8. Stir to mix.
9. Store in the refrigerator and take one shot per day to ward off illness.

New Friends on the Block Spell

Making new friends is always exciting but can also be somewhat anxiety-provoking, as the process of establishing trust begins. For most of us, our friendships are a big part of our lives. They are the people with whom we share and make memories, and who go through our pain and joys with us. I wouldn't be who I am without my friends, and I am sure you feel the same. When meeting a new friend or wishing to make new friends, work this spell and enjoy its results. I will not steer you wrong.

HOW LONG IT TAKES:

24 hours

WHAT YOU'LL NEED:

- 1 bowl or dish of spring water
- 3 rose petals
- Lemon
- 3 sunflower petals
- Rose oil
- Vanilla ice cream

STEPS:

1. In a dish on your altar, float your rose and sunflower petals in some spring water with two drops of rose oil and let it soak until evening. Or, if you plan on

meeting people in the evening, wait until you are ready
to go to bed.

2. Before setting off for work in the morning, drink a
glass of spring water with squeezed lemon.

3. Visualize the lemony light enveloping you from the
inside and illuminating out of your eyes and onto your
face.

4. When you are in a social environment, envision the
light of the lemon coming out of your eyes and notice
how much more alive and interested you feel.

5. Make plans with your new friend(s) to enjoy some
vanilla ice cream together to solidify the friendship.

Cleanse My Spirit Spell

Burning or smudging herbs is a sacred ritual in many ceremonies held for healing and shamanic traditions. It is a way to
cleanse your spirit of negative energies, influences, and vibrations. Burning sacred herbs allows access to the plants' powers,
and their aromas release high levels of vibrational energies to
protect your spiritual and physical bodies. The sacred herbs are
tied into a bundle and then set to dry, making a "smudge
bundle." Treat your bundles with respect.

HOW LONG IT TAKES:

10 days

WHAT YOU'LL NEED:

- String
- Lavender
- Sage
- Sweetgrass
- Cedar
- Palo Santo
- Copal
- Abalone Shell

STEPS:

1. Each one or a combination of the above ingredients

will create your bundle. Feel free to add a bit of lavender to each bundle.

2. Tie each group of herbs at the base with string in a secure knot.

3. Beginning in the center, start wrapping the string toward the top of the bundle and then crisscross the string back to the base.

4. Do not crush the herbs when tying your bundle.

5. Cut off the excess string.

6. Hang your bundles upside down for ten days or more in a cool, dry place.

7. Hold your stick over your abalone shell and evenly light one end. Let it burn for a few moments, and then blow out the flame.

8. Set your intention to cleanse your spirit.

9. Smudge your body from your feet to over your head.

∾

Anxiety Begone Spell

Feelings of anxiety can be so overwhelming that sometimes you have to lie down. It is a necessary defense mechanism, as it warns us of impending danger and triggers hormones necessary for us to fight. Sometimes, we experience anxiety over a simple thought or irrational fear of impending doom. This spell is to rid you of the unhealthy type of anxiety that can be so crippling that it interferes with your quality of life. I thought at one time in my life that I was going to suffer chronic anxiety attacks forever. Not the case! With some exercise, meditation, rituals, and spells, I now live comfortably in my own skin.

HOW LONG IT TAKES:

11 days

WHAT YOU'LL NEED:

- Chamomile
- Honey
- Lavender oil
- White candle
- Wooden toothpick

STEPS:

1. Prepare for yourself a cup of chamomile tea with honey.

2. In the center of your altar, place your white candle and anoint it with lavender oil.

3. Light your candle and meditate while sipping your tea, drawing upon its white light for calmness and relief from anxiety.

4. Sit your tea on your altar next to the candle and chant:

> *I draw upon my power so strong*
> *With it, all anxiety is gone!*
> *No worries, no fear*
> *For peace is now here*
> *As it is and should be*

5. Let the candle burn for five minutes and then snuff it out.

6. Repeat the chant with a cup of tea and a lighted candle for eleven days.

Another Serving of Psychic Intuition, Please Spell

Psychic ability, much like the five senses, gives us information about our surroundings on an energetic and spiritual level. As a witch, I believe that increasing my psychic intuitions is what moves me forward in my spiritual journey.

HOW LONG IT TAKES:

20 minutes

WHAT YOU'LL NEED:

- A spell jar (You can use a regular jar with a lid or a colored jar - it becomes a spell jar after you place your intention upon it.)
- Water
- Salt
- Mint
- Aloe
- Goldenrod
- 1 quarter
- 1 clear quartz crystal
- 1 oxtail bone

STEPS:

1. Place all of your ingredients except the crystal, quarter, and oxtail bone in the bottle.

2. Place your quarter, oxtail bone, and clear quartz crystal in a triangle shape around your spell jar.

3. Imagine silver lights swirling up, down, and around your jar.

4. Focus all of your senses and intentions on enhancing your psychic abilities.

5. Let your energy fill your spell jar.

6. Leave it on your altar overnight to charge.

7. Place it with you wherever you spend time in your house.

8. Place it back on your altar once a week with the bone, quarter, and crystal to recharge.

10

WEALTH SPELLS

Most people are interested in money, especially when struggling to make ends meet. After love magic, money magic is the most common spellwork asked about, and the most commonly practiced after healing spells. As usual, all spells are powered by your intention. A wise witch once told me that while a person's happiness cannot be bought, not having financial burdens certainly makes life easier. I agree that having money also helps us escape many constraints on our energy and time. Time and energy are much better spent on enlightened spiritual pursuits instead of the constant anxieties of finances. Money gives us the autonomy to make decisions about how we choose to live our lives. This chapter will provide you with practical, insightful, and clever spells for changing insubstantial patterns in life to plentiful life patterns in any way you wish to apply your intention. If you find yourself struggling to make it to the end of each month, it is only because you have not yet learned how to attract money. These spells will help you to do just that.

For Richer or Richer Spell

Harnessing moon power is an effective way to attract prosperity. When moon magic and herbal magic work together, it is a recipe for financial success. Basil is often called the abundance herb, and cinnamon the "sweet money herb." Clove, along with cinnamon and basil, raises your spiritual vibrations and amplifies moon magic. This spell is one of my "feel good" spells, too!

HOW LONG IT TAKES:

30 minutes

WHAT YOU'LL NEED:

- Full moon
- Sachet bag
- Cinnamon
- Clove
- Dried basil

STEPS:

1. Cast this spell during a full moon.
2. Place all of the herbs in a sachet bag.
3. Run a warm bath and place the satchet bag into the tub.
4. As you soak in this water during a full moon, envision your spiritual energies rising.

5. As you soak, know, and meditate on your wallet as it fills with money and all of your bills are satisfied.

6. As the water cools, drain your bath.

7. Quickly bury the sachet in the earth under the full moon.

Want Ads New Job Spell

There is always something so exciting yet frightening about looking for a new job. "What if they don't like me?" "Did I do well in the interview?" "Will I have to relocate?" Seeing a job is exciting because it gives rise to new opportunities, widens your network, builds up your resume, and helps you learn new skills. It is the change that is so intimidating. If you want or need a new job and you have anxiety, you're not alone. Anxiety about finding a new job is common but conquerable.

HOW LONG IT TAKES:

50 minutes

WHAT YOU'LL NEED:

- Green fabric
- Needle and green thread
- Pen and paper
- A dollar bill
- Clear quartz crystal (small)
- Allspice
- Cinnamon
- Mint
- Rosemary

STEPS:

1. Using your green fabric, sew together three sides of the sachet.
2. Write down your dream job and some general circumstances for the job you are looking for. Trust in the universe to know what is best. Some examples include "a good salary, good teamwork, use of my creativity."
3. Place into the sachet the herbs, and your paper folded up into a parcel.
4. Add your clear quartz crystal and the dollar bill.
5. Sew your sachet closed.
6. Smudge with sage and chant:

A new job, a good job, is for me
Finding it is as easy as 1, 2, 3
This new job will make me happy as can be
So mote it be

7. Look for the largest tree near your home and bury the sachet near its roots.
8. While you are searching for your job, periodically stop by and water the tree.
9. Happy job hunting and good luck!

Good First Impression Spell

Everyone wants to be remembered. However nice it is to make a good first impression, it also takes some effort on your end. Our need to make a good first impression dates back to prehistoric times, and serves as a defense mechanism by processing information about facial patterns a person exhibits during a first meeting. Our first impression provides us with our feelings about how trustworthy, friendly, honest, and morally sound is the person we are meeting.

HOW LONG IT TAKES:

45 minutes

WHAT YOU'LL NEED:

- 1 whole orange
- 4 tablespoons vanilla extract
- 8 rose petals
- 1½ teaspoons bay leaves
- ½ teaspoon spearmint
- ½ teaspoon peppermint
- ½ teaspoon thyme

STEPS:

1. Draw a warm bath.
2. Place all of the herbs, the rose petals, and vanilla in the water.

3. Cut the orange in half and put it in a bowl next to the tub.

4. Get in the water.

5. Squeeze the juice of ½ the orange into the water.

6. Chant:

> *The first time you meet me, who will I be*
> *A great first impression you will have of me*
> *The day we first meet, I'm sure you will see*
> *You will from now on think highly of me*
> *As it is and should be*

7. Suck the orange out of the other half.

8. Float the orange halves in the water until it starts to cool.

9. Drain the tub and collect the wet ingredients.

10. Scatter them about your yard for the earth and animals to enjoy!

You're Promoted Spell

My first time being promoted felt really good. I felt a sense of worth rooted in hard work. I felt validation for the time and effort I had been putting in. It motivated me by appealing to my ambition. It made me want to achieve even more, and I knew if I added magic to my ambition and motivation, I would work my way to the top. And I did. You can, too, if you set your intentions to match your ambition.

HOW LONG IT TAKES:

10 minutes each morning

WHAT YOU'LL NEED:

- 1 handheld bell
- Ginger
- Patchouli bundle
- Cinnamon sticks
- Clove spice
- Mint (½ cup)
- Gold glitter
- Olive oil (1 cup)
- Frankincense

STEPS:

1. Cleanse your kitchen by smoking the patchouli bundle.

2. Next, add all of the dry ingredients except the gold glitter to a small pot.

3. Add olive oil.

4. Simmer as a potpourri.

5. Each morning sprinkle a pinch of gold glitter in your pot, ring your bell three times, and chant:

> *I work hard, I stay in motion*
> *This week, I will be granted a promotion*
> *Those up the ladder will now notice me*
> *As it is and as it should be!*

6. Do this every day until you receive your promotion.

Debt Free for Me Spell

Have you ever asked yourself, "How did I get here?" Have you found yourself in bondage to your bills? When you get your first loan or credit card, you don't plan on the interest or even making payments. Most people say to themselves, "I am just going to pay it at the end of every month."

HOW LONG IT TAKES:

5+ days

WHAT YOU'LL NEED:

- 1 jar with lid
- Small coins
- Medium-sized coins
- Large coins
- 5 tablespoons flour
- 5 cinnamon sticks
- 5 teaspoons cayenne pepper
- 5 whole pecans

STEPS:

1. Fill up the jar with all the ingredients.
2. Cap it tightly.
3. Shake it and chant:

With the power of these herbs
and the powers that be
My future and now will be debt-free
As it is and should be

4. For the first five days, put the jar in the southwest corner of your kitchen.

5. Then carry the jar with you in a velvet sack wherever you go.

~

Money on the Spot Spell

When I first began my business, I really needed some extra cash. I believed in myself, and I believe in magic, so I started a money bowl. As my business grew, so did my bowl. My goal was to turn a profit within six months of starting it. I hit that goal in two months. Once again, place your intention into each item before putting it in your bowl.

HOW LONG IT TAKES:

One week to one month

WHAT YOU'LL NEED:

- 1 roll of dimes
- Allspice
- Basil
- Wine cork
- Dollar bill
- Money clip
- Old wallet
- Cloves
- Sage
- Green gem
- Green tea candle
- Green cloth
- Anything green and natural

STEPS:

1. Add one dime per day to the bowl.
2. Each day put one ingredient in the bowl along with another dime.
3. Continue this process every day.
4. Your money will grow.

Happy Retirement Spell

Have you ever worried about retirement? How much money do you need? Most people share that boat with you. Depending on their financial status, people retire at all different ages, though most are in their 60's. Some people don't wish to retire until they are unable to work. Perhaps they have not imagined the spiritual journey that retirement affords us. It is by no means for me to judge what a person chooses to do. If you love your job, you never have to work a day in your life. However, for many, they have certainly put in their time and hopefully can look forward to their later years with vibrancy, magic, and much left to learn.

HOW LONG IT TAKES:

Once a month

WHAT YOU'LL NEED:

- Ashwagandha (Winter cherry)
- Turmeric
- Ginseng
- Allspice
- Cumin
- Garlic
- Basil
- 1 silver-colored object
- 1 gold-colored object
- 1 lock of your hair

- 1 jar with lid

STEPS:

1. Prepare your spell jar with the listed ingredients and seal it tightly.
2. On the day of the new moon, take your spell jar with you to a park.
3. Sit on a park bench.
4. Take off your shoes.
5. Start earthing (review chapter six).
6. Chant:

> *I thank the Goddesses*
> *I thank the Gods*
> *I thank myself for working hard*
> *I thank the Elements*
> *I thank the herbs*
> *For giving me the quality of life I deserve*
> *It's not about riches*
> *It's all about love*
> *Love for everyone below and above*
> *In this year now and years to come*
> *I will cherish my garden for giving me love*
> *As it is and should be*

7. Once a month, find a peaceful place for earthing while holding your spell jar. Feel the grass of a golf course, the

sand on the beach, the snow on a mountain, anything that represents things you want to experience when you retire joyfully.

8. Repeat the chant at each place, and it will become sacred and represent a future of retirement beyond your wildest dreams. Believe, as it is and should be.

End My Bad Luck Spell (to banish bad luck)

Have you found yourself chipping a tooth, dropping something heavy on your foot, running out of ink when you just replaced it? I have been there and done that, and it was time to end that string of bad luck. Whether you feel you have just had a string of bad energy or that you may be cursed, this wonderful spell will banish the bad luck you may be experiencing. Before I do this spell, I always take a ritual bath, cleanse, clean and bless my home and myself. I also promise always to follow my intuition and respect my personal signs and intentions.

HOW LONG IT TAKES:

5 hours

WHAT YOU'LL NEED:

- 10" square piece of paper
- Black pen
- Abalone shell
- White candle
- Sage
- Allspice
- Bay leaves

STEPS:

1. In your sacred space, write "BAD LUCK" on a piece of white paper.

2. Under those words, write how bad luck has influenced your life.

3. Draw a large red **X** over each circumstance or experience you wrote about, X-ing them out of your life forever.

4. Imagine yourself safe from harm.

5. Draw a large red **X** over each letter in "BAD LUCK," manifesting your string of bad luck to be banished.

6. Place the herbs in an abalone shell and place the candle on top.

7. Light the candle, light the piece of paper on fire, and drop it into the abalone shell.

8. As the fire burns chant three times:

> *Dark hours, burning fire, my luck improves*
> *by the hour*

9. Once your ingredients have cooled, take ¼ of the ash and scatter it in your toilet, and chant three times:

> *Water on earth running free*
> *I flush this bad luck away from me*

10. Take ¼ more of the ash and throw it in the wind, and chant:

> *Ash in the wind on this dark night*
> *Take my bad luck, and all will be right*

11. Take ¼ more of the ashes and bury them in your garden, and chant:

> **Earth transforms and does not hesitate**
> **Remove my bad luck, for I do not relate**

12. Carry the last ¼ of the ash in a baggie and empty it out of the window of a car when you are as far from your house as possible and chant:

> **As it is and should be**

A Path to New Opportunities Spell

I hate to be the one to tell you, but new opportunities don't just land in your lap. They require you to find ways to attract them into your life. Along with your magic, you have to put yourself out there. Being open-minded and in touch with your energy will empower your magic to open your eyes to opportunities when they arise. They can come in many forms. They may be small opportunities like lending a helping hand or big opportunities like a new job. Or huge opportunities, like getting to take a ride on a space shuttle. After you cast this spell, you just have to notice them, and it will seem like they fell into your lap.

HOW LONG IT TAKES:

30 minutes

WHAT YOU'LL NEED:

- Fire-safe bowl
- Matches
- Charcoal
- Feather
- 1 tablespoon crushed camomile leaves
- 1 teaspoon cinnamon
- ½ teaspoon ginger
- ½ teaspoon bay leaves

STEPS:

1. Mix all of the ingredients in the fire-safe bowl.

2. Close your eyes and envision yourself walking down a hallway of an ancient house to a very old door. The old door represents any obstacles or anything blocking you from new opportunities.

3. Imagine yourself opening the door, and a brilliant light flows in and covers you.

4. Meditate on the freedom you feel facing a world of new opportunities and chant:

> *Opportunities are new*
> *Coming out of the blue*
> *Sacred brilliant light*
> *Has removed all of my fright*
> *Onward I march without any fear*
> *I thank my herbs, and hold them dear.*

5. Place the charcoal atop the herbs and light it.

6. Fan yourself with the smoke using a feather and chant:

> *As it is and should be*

Shamrock Good Luck Spell

The luck of the shamrock dates back to Celtic priests known as the Druids in the early times of Ireland. They believed that carrying a shamrock, or three-leaf clover enabled them to foresee evil spirits, providing them time to escape. For the Celtics, by 1620, four-leaf clovers were thought of as magical charms to keep away bad luck. During the middle ages, children believed they would see fairies if they were to carry a four-leaf clover. This discussion first appeared in a text by Sir. John Melton in 1620, in which he suggested they bring good fortune[1]. I believe those children saw fairies because they intended to see fairies and believed in fairies. Good luck has to be believed in for this spell to work. Intention has to be truthful for any spell to work.

HOW LONG IT TAKES:

30-45 minutes

WHAT YOU'LL NEED:

- A shiny new penny
- A white candle
- Abalone shell
- A drawing of a four leaf clover
- Spearmint or mint leaves

STEPS:

1. Cleanse your altar.

2. Light the white candle.

3. Place your mint leaves in your abalone shell.

4. Flip the penny onto your altar until it lands on heads three times in a row. It may take a while, but eventually, it happens.

5. Burn your drawing atop your herbs in your abalone shell and chant:

> *Luck of the shamrock, send luck to me*
> *With this offering*
> *As it is and should be*

6. Let the candle burn all the way down.

FINAL THOUGHTS

If you are new to spellcrafting with herbs, know this: spells are cast, and rituals are performed every day by many people. Understanding how important it is to have positive energy is vital to raising your spiritual vibrations. You have made a connection with each herb by learning everything you can about them. The more confidence you have in your spells, the more powerful they become and the faster your results. Herbal magic takes time, patience, love, and understanding. So, there is a bit more to green magic than one may practice with candles or crystals. All three together make for powerful, strong magic, and you do not have to grow your candles or water your crystals. I love it because the watering, feeding, providing the right amount of sunlight and knowing when to harvest their leaves, roots, stems, flowers, and their essences all create a bond that is much like the one I have with my closest friends. Tapping into your inner strength for empowerment is essential to magic-making. Learning the techniques of herbal magic will enable you to master your spellcraft and fulfill your destiny of becoming a skilled practitioner! Your effort and patience will greatly reward you if you focus your intention, believe in your spell, and keep your focus during the session. Focus, intent, and belief are the core ingredients to all spells.

Detailed in this book are herbs' magical history, folklore, recipes, elixirs, jar spells, bathing rituals, and much more. Pagan Sabbats or holidays are set to the earth's natural rhythms and seasons. The Sabbats detailed in this book celebrate the earth's journey around the sun, known as the Wheel of the Year, and the celebrations commemorating the Sabbats are referred to as Turning the Wheel. Also provided is a step-by-step guide for casting a sacred circle. In its fundamental form, a sacred circle can be a space visualized by you or can be designed with your ritual tools and created within and around your altar, outside, or anywhere you cast it for spellcrafting. Most magical workers believe their sacred circle is an energy container, and they practice their craft from within it. It is a spiritual shield protecting you from all negativity during the deeply emotional and vulnerable state you have to be in for your spells to work. It is like an invisible, impenetrable force field, from which negativity, imbalance, and disharmony bounce off.

In this book, you are provided with powerful love spells that so many people have come to me for. When people come to me for love magic, they are full of the power of positive thinking and trust in the process. I hope you feel the same. Practicing love spells is about - you guessed it - Love! Here is the deal; love spells work much more efficiently if the energy is already there and headed in a specific direction. Therefore, if the feelings budding are mutual, magic helps to accelerate the feelings, emotions, vibrations, and energies between the two people involved. It works like a magnetic force field pulling two people together. It is about attracting rather than making someone love you. Keep an open heart and mind while casting love spells. Sometimes they deliver more than you bargained for, but in a good way.

The money spells provided to you are designed to meet your specific individual needs, whether you are job hunting, need to improve your finances, preparing for retirement, or even to nudge along a business transaction. I shared these particular spells intending to help those looking for magical resources, and you may want to adjust them to meet your individual needs. Herbs have been used for centuries to amplify money spells. Money in its basic form is a tool you use for the trade of services or goods. However, it does contain energy, as in "the flow of money." The only time money becomes a problem in life is when you do not have enough of it to meet your needs or when you start hoarding it instead of saving it. When you become so worried about spending a penny, you are basically shouting out to the universe that you don't trust that it has your back. Hence, you block the energy flow of money.

To know thyself is the first rule of witchcraft. That includes understanding your relationship with money, how it developed, and which herbs work best for you in your prosperity spells. This book contains detailed information on the correspondence between money and basil, clove, rosemary, ginger, sage, and others, which have been used in spellwork and for trade throughout history. Remember, some herbs are not edible, so err on the side of caution. You can make powders by grinding up herbs with your mortar and pestle and then making magical blends. Roll your candles in herbs, add them to your money jar or mojo bag, add a stick of cinnamon or some basil in your coin purse or wallet for a bit of daily money magic.

Herbs have been a part of healing magic from the Stone Age and ancient societies all the way up to modern times. Western medicine's origins lie in the early healing lore of sedentary farmers, Paleolithic hunters and gathers, and herding nomads, rather than in traditional academically-based pharmacists and doctors. Healing with herbs is an integral aspect of this book and the many ways people from ancient times and today have used herbs in their surrounding environment. Traditions and knowledge that have been handed down to treat various conditions and ailments encountered in our daily lives are a priceless part of the magic kingdom. In writing this book, I realized the truest magic in all worlds is the opportunity to make a difference in someone's life. I hope this knowledge and these spells do that for you!

NOTES

1. THE MAGIC OF HERBS

1. The World Health Organization. WHO Traditional Medicine Strategy: 2014–23. 2013. 6 August 2018. http://apps.who.int/medicinedocs/en/m/abstract/Js21201en/

4. ESSENTIAL HERBS

1. https://garden.org/ideas/view/Sharon/982/Looking-for-Magic-Cayenne-Pepper/
2. https://www.thespruceeats.com/history-of-cinnamon-1807584
3. https://www.bowerandbranch.com/the-legend-of-the-dogwood/#:~:text=A%20dogwood.,again%20be%20used%20in%20crucifixion

9. HEALTH SPELLS

1. https://www.ncbi.nlm.nih.gov/pmc/articles/PMC4020364/

10. WEALTH SPELLS

1. https://sctlandtrust.org/2020/03/17/history-of-the-four-leaf-clover-clover-crafts/#:~:text=The%20Druids%20(Celtic%20-priests)%2C,and%20ward%20off%20bad%20luck.

Made in the USA
Las Vegas, NV
08 November 2024

11303621R00105